Train Your
MINDSET
Accept No Excuses In the Game of Life

COACH GATLIN

authorHOUSE®

AuthorHouse™
1663 Liberty Drive
Bloomington, IN 47403
www.authorhouse.com
Phone: 1 (800) 839-8640

Published by AuthorHouse 03/18/2020

ISBN: 978-1-7283-4744-8 (sc)
ISBN: 978-1-7283-4743-1 (hc)
ISBN: 978-1-7283-4829-2 (e)

Library of Congress Control Number: 2020905309

Print information available on the last page.

This collection of writings by Mr. Gatlin holds many life lessons to learn from, to grow from, and obstacles to overcome. This book holds many inspirational stories, quotes, and thoughts that can guide you to the next step in your life journey. The lessons taught in this book are there for you to grasp; you just have to be willing to change your way of thinking and doing.

— Dr. Regina Tillman

"Fred Gatlin's *Train Your Mindset* is helpful, practical, and relevant – demonstrating how mindsets shape who we are and how we can do a better job of leading others in all facades of life."

— Dr. Tu Price

Contents

~SECOND HALF~

Introduction

The Two Friends Deep Within

Our minds have opportunities every day to be vulnerable, strong, simple, and complex. Training our mind-set is a daily battle of the two friends within who live inside of us. One friend is phenomenal, sharp, and confident. This is the friend who is willing to explore and learn new things. The other friend is common, average, and scared to put in the necessary work to be great. This friend is in survival mode. This is the friend who is fighting to protect you by any means necessary. This friend fights to protect you from hard/uncomfortable work and keep you in your comfort zone. Whichever one we feed and train the most will always win the battle of the day. Every morning we wake up, the battle begins.

This concrete wilderness we live in is full of pain and suffering or joy and happiness. The weapons (good information versus bad information) we choose to use in this wilderness can either hurt us or make us stronger and wiser.

Excuses

We all make excuses at some point in our lives because excuses are what make us feel safe, protected, and very comfortable. If we're completely honest with ourselves, excuses simply keep us locked into our mental realm of mediocrity.

What excuses are you making on a daily, weekly, or monthly basis that keep you in your comfort zone? I guarantee you that whatever those excuses are, they are definitely holding you back from what truly belongs to you. The battle between the two friends within starts the moment we open our eyes each morning. Decisions, decisions, decisions. Which friend will you feed, and which one will you starve today?

The journey you will take throughout this book will make you laugh, make you think, and hopefully give you hope. Some stories will be exactly for you and others will be for someone who is close to you. Train your mind until it hurts, and eventually, it will respond at its best when your best is needed!

The two friends within will battle, but the one
who is fed the most will always win!

Something for you to think about as a reader is that there are two types of people in this world: those who read books like this and do nothing and those who put what they read into practice and enjoy immediate results.

~Phil M. Jones

~FIRST HALF~

I Don't Have Time to Read This Book

1

If you create the time and courage to read past this first paragraph, I guarantee you'll find something that will spark a flame inside of you. If you don't read past this first paragraph, you will never receive the gift that was put somewhere in this book especially for you. If you keep reading, you will instantly start to recognize the excuses that title each chapter. These are excuses that many of us have relied so heavily on at different stages in our lives. It's time to break them down and stop letting them control us. It's time for us to search and find the best versions of ourselves each and every day.

There had to be something about the cover that sparked your interest. Out of all of the books you had to choose from, you find yourself with this one in your possession. So, you might as well keep reading, so your mind-set can start the shift that it needs.

I believe excuses are lies that we as human beings create to protect ourselves from discomfort. We use excuses to protect ourselves from struggle, pain, and the unknown. We oftentimes use excuses because we're too comfortable with the lives we've already created for ourselves. Are you satisfied with your life or with your current situation at this very moment?

It's time to challenge all of the excuses that pertain to you. This book may even bring to the surface some excuses you need to battle that are not included in this book. You have already taken the first step toward changing your mind-set by beginning this first chapter. It's time to go get your gifts that God created just for you. It's also time to develop those gifts and bless the world with them.

These pages are filled with personal stories, quotes, history, and data that will make you think, make you laugh, make you angry, make you share, and force you to be accountable for your life and the decisions made or not made in the past. These pages will force you to be accountable for the decisions and actions you need to take in the near future. They will also force you to surround yourself with a positive team of supporters because, for most of us, it's hard to do anything worthwhile by ourselves.

This book is for you if you're thirteen, seventeen, twenty-five, forty, or even eighty. These pages do not discriminate! This book is for anyone who is mature enough and ready to change his or her mind-set and change his or her life by an inch. An inch is the difference between someone who is rich and someone who is broke. The word *rich* is very relative for many of us. It just depends on who you're talking to. To some, rich could mean:

- ❖ Having a hundred dollars or a million dollars
- ❖ Having something to eat every day or once a week
- ❖ Getting your first job or the job of your dreams
- ❖ Getting your first apartment or the house of your dreams
- ❖ Gaining a quality relationship with loved ones for the first time
- ❖ Losing weight
- ❖ Gaining muscle
- ❖ Learning how to read or write
- ❖ Stopping negative and addictive behavior
- ❖ Finding hope and faith
- ❖ Going to college, going back to college, or even being the first in your family to go to college
- ❖ Making the team
- ❖ Getting a promotion

It's time for us to stop being mentally, spiritually, psychologically, and financially broke and broken. These pages will help lead you to wherever it is you need to go. These pages will help you find that inch you need to gain. It's time to change your mind-set today and for the rest of your life.

If you continue to explore these pages, you will start to unlock some of the love you've been holding back from yourself. You will unlock the potential happiness that's waiting for you on the other side of self-discipline.

Now, your mission is to read the rest of this book and start the tough journey of thinking, imagining, planning and eventually doing so you can live like a true champion. If you choose to accept this mission, the keys you need to unlock the door will be waiting inside the following chapters.

Life is a competition between you and you; the you that wants to work hard for positive change, and the you that wants to stay in your comfort zone.

~ Ray Lewis, two-time Super Bowl champion
linebacker and Hall of Famer, #52

~Notes~

1

All of My Friends Are Doing It!

2

One of my favorite sayings to my students is, "I don't care if you're twelve or sixty-five! Whoever you hang out with the most is going to influence you the most." If we stop for a second and look at the top five people we associate with the most, we'll really be able to see a good reflection of ourselves.

For example, If your top five are saving money, going to study hall, helping at the homeless shelter, playing sports, going to the gym, investing in real estate, going to college, or going to church, you will most likely be right there with them.

On the other hand, if your top five are always getting high on drugs, running the streets, drinking, playing video games, gossiping, finding themselves broke, spending time on social media, or ending up in some type of drama, just look at them, and you'll see your reflection staring right back at you. You will always be as financially, mentally, or spiritually broken as they are. If your top five are lazy and have no work ethic, please pack your bags and run.

If you look deep into the mirror, you will always see what you need to see about your current state of being. Do me a favor and look at your appearance, look at your surroundings, look at your habits, and look at your actions. Once you see what you need to see, you will have the information you need to make an informed decision on what group of people you need to run from or what group of people you need run toward or stay in contact with.

One of my mentors once told me, "If you're the smartest person in your group, then you're in the wrong group; and if four people in your group are broke, you will soon be the fifth!" We must be able to learn from those in our immediate circle. We should not be the 'all wise one' all of the time. If your inner circle of friends are consistently taking from you, you will always feel drained and have nothing left to give for yourself. Your inner circle should be able to give as much as they take from you.

If all of your friends are doing it, it's either going to continue to kill you and keep you further away from being an exceptional human being, or it's going to continue to push you in the right direction of growth and prosperity. Please take a moment to look in the mirror. Your mirror is with you every day.

- ❖ It's in your contacts.
- ❖ It's talking to you on the phone.
- ❖ It's texting you.
- ❖ It's on Instagram or Facebook with you.
- ❖ It's smoking weed with you.
- ❖ It's drinking alcohol with you.
- ❖ It's at the club with you.
- ❖ It's gangbanging with you.
- ❖ It's gossiping with you.
- ❖ It's walking with you in the mall.
- ❖ It's on your team.
- ❖ It's sitting down at the business meeting with you.
- ❖ It's at the seminar with you.
- ❖ It's pumping iron at the gym with you.
- ❖ It's running stadium bleachers with you.
- ❖ It's studying with you.
- ❖ It's eating lunch with you.
- ❖ It's in the passenger seat next to you.

❖ It's watching the game with you or maybe even making a million-dollar deal with you.

If we just look carefully, we'll always see ourselves staring right back at us.

No matter if you're twelve or sixty-five, whoever you hang out with the most is going to influence you the most, good or bad.

~Notes~

2

I'm Too Tall Young Ladies

3

I hear this a lot from a variety of my female students who are taller than most of their peers. They say they don't want to stand out. They don't want people looking at them all of the time. They also tend to walk around campus with their shoulders slumped over to make themselves look smaller. They refuse to walk with their shoulders back and head held high with confidence.

One young lady came to my office crying one day because she was tired of everyone teasing her about her height. She was thirteen years old, five eleven, and probably about 165 pounds. It was heartbreaking to see how much society, social media, magazines, music videos, songs, sitcoms, and, of course, her peers had destroyed her self-image.

I tried my best to assure her that she was a beautiful little girl just the way she was. I asked her who she loved and respected. She told me her mom and grandmother. I said, "That's great! These are the people who created you. You are a spitting image of them. These are the women who raised you. These are the women who put a roof over your head. They buy the groceries. They buy your clothes and give you money when you need it, and they give you discipline, advice and instruction, when you need it the most."

I also said, "If you love and respect them, then you should love and respect what you look like and who you are." I already know the next question: "What if she didn't respect or love them?" I say, look and learn from other great women who have demonstrated great effort and sacrifice to create the best versions of themselves. Look for women who have inspired and helped others along the way. Find women whom you admire and study them. Study their courage and work ethic. Study their grace, their beauty, their ambition, and, last but not least, the confidence they have in themselves.

Back to my former student. I took it upon myself to go home and create a small five-page booklet for her of all of the tall women I could think of who have made great contributions to their chosen craft and the world. The goal was to show her different women who look like her and have made the world a better place with their service to others. I wanted to show her just a sample of the many powerful women in the world who have embraced themselves and have become confident women that little girls can look up to and aspire to be one day. Here are a few of the names that were in the booklet. All of the information about these powerful women is constantly changing. If you don't know what these powerful women look like, please take out your phone and search for them online as you read. Due to certain copyright laws, I was unable to put their pictures in my book.

Michelle Obama, 5' 11"

- First Lady of the United States of America 2008–2016
- Lawyer
- Author
- Advocate for healthy families, higher education, and international adolescent girls education
- Launched Joining Forces, a nationwide initiative calling on all Americans to rally around service members, veterans, and their families.
- Graduate of Harvard Law School

Beyoncé, 5' 7"

- Net worth: $450 million
- Recording artist, songwriter, actress, choreographer, and fashion designer
- 20 Grammy Awards
- 24 MTV Video Music Awards
- 10 films

Serena Williams, 5' 9"

- Professional tennis player
- Prize money from wins: $82 million
- 22 Grand Slam titles
- 38 major titles
- 4 Olympic gold medals
- Fashion designer
- Actress

Venus Williams, 6' 1"

- Professional tennis player
- Prize money from wins: $34 million
- 7 Grand Slam titles
- 49 singles titles
- 4 Olympic gold medals
- Fashion designer
- Ambassador for women's tennis. Fought for equal pay for women in her sport. Women now get the same prize money as men because of her play and her voice.

Candace Parker, 6' 4"

- WNBA player for the Los Angeles Sparks
- 2016 WNBA champion
- Finals MVP
- 2 Olympic gold medals

- 2008 Rookie of the Year

Oprah Winfrey, 5' 7"

- Net worth: $2.9 Billion
- CEO of Harpo Productions
- Former host of *The Oprah Winfrey Show*
- CEO of *OWN Magazine*
- CEO of OWN Network
- Actress
- Author
- Raped at the age of nine and sexually abused from the ages of ten to fourteen
- Pregnant at the age of fourteen and lost her baby two weeks after he was born
- Physically beaten and abused as a child
- Still standing *tall*!

Rihanna, 5' 8"

- Singer, songwriter, fashion designer, model, and actress
- Net worth: $160 million
- 200 million records sold worldwide
- 8 Grammy Awards
- 12 American Music Awards
- 12 Billboard Music Awards
- 4 films

Lisa Leslie, 6' 5"

- Former WNBA player for the Los Angeles Sparks (1997–2009)
- Studio analyst
- Head coach with the BIG3 Professional Basketball League
- Model
- Actor
- 2 WNBA championships and three finals MVPs
- Three WNBA MVPs

- 8 WNBA All-Star selections
- 4 Olympic gold medals
- Basketball Hall of Famer (enshrined in 2015)
- Net worth: $5 million

Queen Latifah, 5' 10"

- Singer, rapper, record producer, talk show host, actress, songwriter, and speech composer
- 7 albums
- 40-plus films
- 21 television shows
- 11 NAACP Awards
- 8 BET Awards
- Net worth: $60 million

Other tall little girls you might want to look up and study include:
- Kimora Lee Simmons, 6' 2"
- Famke Janssen, 6'
- Tyra Banks, 5' 10"
- Gisele Bundchen, 5' 11"
- Nicole Kidman, 5' 11"
- Taylor Swift, 5' 10"
- Jordin Sparks, 5' 10"
- Khloé Kardashian, 5' 10"
- Chrissy Teigen, 5' 9"

These are just a few of the many tall girls who grew up to become powerful women. To the young ladies who are reading this: Stand tall and become a giant in this world. Don't be ashamed of the way God made you. He made you that way for a reason. Walk with confidence, with your shoulders back and your head held high. You can be an inspiration to someone in your family, your school, or your neighborhood or even to someone on the other side of the world one day. Be the best person you can be, and strive to be great every day, young lady. Average is not an option.

As my mentor (from YouTube) Dr. Eric Thomas always says, "Be a lion not a gazelle. Lions hunt for greatness! Gazelles run from it!"

To Us Adults

Our little girls have way too much stress put on them regarding their body image. No matter if they're tall, short, thin, or plus size, they get it from all sides. They hear it from the girls, boys, magazines, videos, movies, certain rap songs, and the internet. We all need to do our part to help build their self-esteem so they can grow into the people they were put on this earth to be. Let's work together to stir them in the right direction, so they can start healing and growing.

You're beautiful just the way God made you. Embrace you!

~Notes~

3

_____
_____
_____
_____
_____
_____
_____
_____
_____
_____
_____
_____
_____
_____
_____
_____
_____
_____
_____
_____
_____
_____
_____
_____

It Takes Too Long

4

I hope you truly understand that anything worth having and sustaining is going to take time to develop and grow. It's going to take hard work, dedication, and more than a few days of pain and suffering before you see the fruits of your labor. Let's look at a few of these words a little more closely.

Work (verb): Exertion or effort directed to produce or accomplish something; labor; toil.

Dedication (dedicate, verb): To devote wholly and earnestly, as to some person or purpose.

Pain (noun): Physical suffering or distress, as due to injury, illness, etc.

Suffering (suffer, verb): To undergo or feel pain or distress. To sustain injury, disadvantage, or loss.

Develop (verb): To cause to grow or expand.

Grow (verb): To increase gradually in size, amount, etc.; become greater or larger; expand.

Labor (verb): Productive activity, physical or mental work, especially of a hard or fatiguing kind; toil.

Fruit (noun): Anything produced or accruing; product, result, or effect; return or profit.

I believe it's always good to slow down and really study certain words so we can really digest them. Sometimes we really need to understand what they mean, so we can use them to help change our behavior. The more we expand our vocabulary, the more we start to understand the world we experience on a daily basis. Our minds begin to open up like parachutes, but I digress. Back to the subject at hand.

I constantly tell my students and athletes I train, "The only time success comes before work is in the dictionary!" We live in a time when we can get everything we want at the push of a button. Technology has made things so easy for us. In my opinion, technology has helped handicap an entire generation of young people—and adults, for that matter. A lot of young people think the world owes them something. Some of them think everything is going to come easily because of the instant gratification that they often get from technology and their parents. Here's the problem. Kids (not all, but a lot) get home and see the big house, the cars in the driveway, the clothes and shoes in the closet, and the food in the refrigerator, and they take it for granted. They tend to easily forget that they did not work one bit for any of that stuff. They forget so easily because they have $800 cell phones and $150 pairs of shoes in their closets. So they become accustomed to that lifestyle. Work ethic, accountability, and responsibility just fall to the wayside. Of course, there are exceptions to the rule, but for the most part, a lot of kids are being set up for a big slap in the face in the future. When it's really time to work for what they need or want, the pressure eats many of them alive, and they just fall apart.

I didn't get my first phone until I was twenty-one years old. Why? Because I had to wait until I could afford one. No one just gave me free technology. As a teenager in the late eighties and early nineties, that was unheard of. Don't get me wrong, as a sneaky teenager, I definitely asked for a (land line) phone for my room, but my aunt was old-school so she would say, "Hell no! You don't need no damn phone in that room. You just want to be on the phone all night with those pissing-tale girls!" And that was that! No phone. You can walk around nowadays and see six-year-olds with iPhones. What?! Try to give a teenager a flip phone today, and he'll throw it back in your face. I've even heard some teenagers have the nerve to say, "A flip phone? Please! It's too embarrassing to be seen with that ancient technology!"

I ask students what they want to be when they grow up. Many of my boys say, "I want to be a professional football or basketball player." I then ask them, "How many jumpers did you shoot yesterday? Did you work on your left hand? How many push-ups did you do last night? How many balls did you catch yesterday? Do you have a 3.0 GPA?"

The answers from all of them are ridiculous!

"I shot 10 jumpers yesterday."

"My homework is too hard."

"My classes are boring."

"I didn't do anything this week."

"I did twenty push-ups this week."

"I was at my aunt's house all week."

"I was at my friend's house playing video games."

"I have too much homework."

It's just ridiculous. I always share with them that Koby Bryant would get up at three o'clock in the morning to shoot and make between two hundred to 1,000 jumpers, and he already had three championship rings at the time. I tell my athletes straight out: You don't want to go to the NBA or the NFL! You have no work ethic, son. If you want to make it to the show, you're going to have to put in the work on and off the field. You have to be obsessed! You have to dream about it every day! Smell it! Eat it! Think it and study it every day! You have to work on your craft and skill every single day! Some nights you're going to have to stay up until one o'clock in the morning doing homework because you practiced for two, three, or four hours after school. You may have to wake up at three o'clock in the morning because that is the best time for you to put in the extra work you need. What are you willing to sacrifice in order to get what you really want?

Sacrifice. Here's another vocabulary word.

Sacrifice (verb): The surrender or destruction of something prized or desirable for the sake of something considered as having a higher or more pressing claim.

I was fortunate enough to learn early on that if we get something too easy, we can never really appreciate that thing like we should. It doesn't mean much to us. We don't give it much value. It meets our needs for a short while, and then we're done with it. Think about it. Think back and be honest with yourself. Think about all of the things in your life that were given to you or came too easily. We either discarded it, took it for granted, or lost it.

It's impossible for us to really value something we didn't work for, as opposed to something we had to work and grind to get. If we have to grind to get it, we protect it. We learn from it. We build from it. We develop it. That experience teaches us and reminds us that we have to work even harder for other things that we need and want later on in life.

Anything worth having and sustaining is going
to take time to develop and grow.

~Notes~

4

I Need My Sleep

5

One of my favorite quotes come from my mentor (from a far), Dr. Thomas. He says, "Sleep is the new broke!" I'm going to let you process that one for a minute. This one single quote has helped transform the structure of my life. This quote is the first thing you see hanging up in my office when you walk in. He reminds me that we only have twenty-four hours in a day. What are you going to do with it? There's so much that needs to get done in the course of a day. My goal is to be the best at whatever I'm doing or trying to accomplish. I know I have to be allergic to average on a daily basis if I want to see improvement and growth in all aspects of my life.

Get Up Early

Those who are successful get up early to start their grind. I used to get up in just enough time to get to work. I was wasting valuable time I could've been using to improve myself. Here's an example of what one of my days may look like when I was coaching and working on this book.

2:00–2:15 a.m. – pray and meditate

2:30–4:30 a.m. – breakfast, work on book

5:00–5:45 a.m. – gym

6:15 a.m. – off to work

6:45 a.m.–4:30 p.m. – work day

2:30–4:00 p.m. – head coach basketball practice

5:30–7:00 p.m. – golf range and putting (training for upcoming tournaments)

7:00–10:00 p.m. – home (family time)

Writing out a schedule for the day has proved to help me stay organized and committed to what is on my schedule. I know if I write it down, I have no excuse for not getting it done. Think of it as a grocery list. When you write out a grocery list and you're walking around the grocery store, you don't leave the store until everything is scratched off the list. *Boom!* I look at my list and scratch off what needs to get done, and I move to the next task or appointment. Nine times out of ten, if you schedule it and keep the schedule handy and visible, you will get it done.

CEOs Who Wake Up between 3:00 a.m. and 5:00 a.m. Every Morning

- Dr. Eric Thomas, motivational speaker, author, professor
- Tim Cook, Apple
- Robert Iger, Disney
- Brett Yormark, former CEO of New Jersey Nets
- Andrea Jung, former CEO of Avon Products
- Howard Schultz, former CEO of Starbucks
- 50 Cent, rapper, producer, actor, creator of *Power* drama series
- Steve Harvey, *The Steve Harvey Show*, The Steve Harvey Radio Show, *Family Feud* host, Miss Universe host
- Kobe Bryant, five-time NBA champion (Rest in Peace!)
- Single parents, CEOs of their homes

I could write a list of at least twenty more pages if I wanted to. I'm sure you get the point by this short list of giants.

Get up! Get up physically, as well as mentally. If you don't do it, who will? If not now, when? Dr. Thomas reminds us that, "You have to want to succeed, as bad as you want to breathe!"

One of my favorite movie franchise of all time is *Rocky*. *Rocky I* through *Rocky IV* were off the chain! Code switch: For those not well versed in slang, that means *Rocky I* through *Rocky IV* were exceptional! My favorite movie from the franchise is *Rocky III*. Rocky goes back to the hood to be trained by Apollo Creed for his upcoming rematch with Clubber Lang (played by Mr. T). My favorite scene is when Rocky is in the ring training with Apollo, and he's sleepwalking through the sparing session. I'm going to set up the scene for you and then walk you through it.

"There Is No Tomorrow" *Rocky III* (1982)

Rocky and Apollo are sparing in the ring. Apollo has Rocky up against the ropes and is talking to him as he's jabbing. (Apollo is training Rocky for the biggest fight of his life.)

Apollo: Watch it now. Watch it. Now remember. He has two hands, right?

(He keeps jabbing Rocky, but Rocky is just standing there taking a beating. Apollo stops jabbing and starts yelling at Rocky.)

Apollo: Damn, man! What the hell are you doing? This guy will knock you on your ass. Come on, Rock! This is not a game! You want to live in the hospital for five weeks this time? You thought I was tough? This chump will kill you!

Rocky: (speaking very lethargic) All right.

(The sparing session continues. Apollo starts talking to Rocky again before he starts throwing punches.)

Apollo: Come on. Come on. Get your head out of your shoulders, man. Think about the fight! Think about the fight! Clubber Lang, he's trying to hurt you, Rock! He's trying to hurt you! Okay, here it comes. Jab … He's jabbing. (Apollo starts punching Rocky while he's talking.) He's jabbing. He's trying to hurt you! You got to fight 'im. You got to move!

(Rocky just stands there and takes the punishment, hit after hit! He's standing there taking a beating, as he thinks about Clubber Lang punishing him in the first fight they had. Apollo then gives him three hooks in a row.)

Apollo: (talking to Rocky as he's throwing hooks at him) He's hooking! He's hooking! He's hooking! (Apollo stops punching him.) Damn, Rock, come on! What's the matter with you?

Rocky: (speaking faintly) Tomorrow.

Apollo: *There is no tomorrow! There is no tomorrow!*

(The scene cuts to Rocky looking in the mirror after the sparing session as those words echo in his head: *There is no tomorrow!*)

If you have never seen this movie, please go buy it or at least search YouTube for this scene. Type in: **Rocky III – Apollo Creed – "There is no tomorrow!"**

In my opinion, this has got to be one of the best scenes in movie history. Clubber Lang represents everything we're scared of, everything we want to run from, and everything that is backing us into a corner and has us paralyzed day after day. We keep taking that beating at work. We keep taking that beating at home. We keep taking that beating in practice. We keep taking that beating with our finances. We keep taking that beating with our credit. We keep taking that beating from bullies. We keep taking that beating from our friends. We keep taking that beating from our kids, from our spouses, and from our dreams and goals that keep haunting us because we've done nothing or we've stopped pursuing them. We either consciously or unconsciously keep taking a beating from average and below average behavior!

If we want to be champions, we are going to have to fight back! When we fight back, we gain confidence each and every jab. We just need to throw the first punch and continue to keep punching our way out of the corner we've been standing and sleeping in for so long. Some of us are sleeping with our eyes closed, and others of us are sleeping with our eyes wide open. Either way, *you're asleep.* It's time to get up because *there is no tomorrow!*

Remember what Dr. Thomas said: "Sleep is the new broke!"

Broke (adjective): Having completely run out of money, fractured, split, divided.

Synonyms: penniless, moneyless, bankrupt, ruined, down-and-out, without a cent, without two pennies to rub together

Please remember: Money is not the only thing we let slip through our fingers when we're sleeping too long. It could be a relationship, a job opportunity, a chance to make a team, a chance to get into school, a chance to invest, a chance to create, or a chance to meet someone of great influence. Remember, today is all we have. *There is no tomorrow!*

There is no tomorrow!

~ Apollo Creed, *Rocky III*

~Notes~

5

_____
_____
_____
_____
_____
_____
_____
_____
_____
_____
_____
_____
_____
_____
_____
_____
_____
_____
_____
_____
_____

Everyone Will Think I'm Crazy

6

The question we have to ask ourselves is, "Am I doing this for me or for someone else?" If you're doing something for yourself, then what others think should not matter to you. If you're doing something for others, you will always care about what they think. If you have a dream or an idea and feel passionate about it, you must jump off of the ledge, as Steve Harvey says, and worry about the results of the landing once you hit the ground.

You may be afraid that everyone will think you're crazy. You're exactly right! Anything that other people don't want to do or are scared to do or that looks impossible to do will be viewed as crazy. The only person who shouldn't think it's crazy is you and maybe a select few who you trust with your vision. These select few should support your craziness 100 percent. If you haven't noticed yet, I love lists, so let me list a few crazy people for you. You might just recognize a few people on this ridiculous list.

Zion Shaver Clark ~ High School and Collegiate Wrestler with No Legs

Zion Shaver Clark was born in 1997 with no legs. He had caudal regression syndrome, which is a condition that affects the development of the lower half of the body. He was put up for adoption soon after he was born. Although he was bounced around from home to home, being starved and beaten, wrestling was the one thing that was steady in his life since the age of seven. His determination and drive to succeed pushed him throughout his life to be the best at whatever he put his mind to. During his senior year at Massillon Washington High School in Ohio, his wrestling record was 33–15. He was just crazy enough to believe that he could wrestle at any level. In 2019 he was a student athlete at Kent State where he was a proud member of their wrestling team and competed in track and field. In addition, he is a strong contender for the US Paralympic team for sprint cycling in 2020. I'll bet my house that this student athlete will make it and make it big.

David Goggins ~ Former Navy Seal Chief

During his early military career, military doctors informed David that he had sickle cell anemia and gave him the option to drop out. Training was extremely hard, and he was very uncomfortable with water, so he quit. He left the military and gained a lot of weight, eventually finding himself at 297 pounds. After a few years of dead-end jobs, he decided to change his life. He actually was able to find a recruiter who was willing to give him a shot at 297 pounds. Incredibly, he was able to lose 106 pounds in three months and changed his life forever.

This former Navy Seal Chief failed boot camp twice with stress fractures and pneumonia the first go-round and a fractured kneecap the second. Unfortunately, he had to roll back to day one of boot camp twice, but, with pure determination, he unconsciously endured Navy Seal hell weeks back-to-back and made it through. Not only did he complete Navy Seal training, but he also completed Army Ranger School and Air Force Tactical Air Controller training. With all of this training, he was able to partake in the Afghanistan and Iraq wars.

In 2019, he was an ultramarathon runner, ultra-distance cyclist, and triathlete. He once ran 100 miles in 19 hours. He also ran 135 miles in just under 26 hours. He has completed more than 60 ultramarathons, and as of 2019, he held the Guinness World Record for most pull-ups done in 24 hours—more than 4,000! Please read his book *Can't Hurt Me*. It's estimated his net worth is $260,000, but I say his net worth is priceless.

Wilbur and Orville Wright ~ Inventors

The Wright brothers were the inventors of the three-axis control, which enabled pilots to steer an aircraft effectively and maintain its equilibrium. Let's fast-forward from 1903 to present day. Now we have airlines that take us all across the world. Southwest, Delta, United, American, Frontier, Spirit, Alaska, Virgin, Hawaiian, JetBlue—there are too many to mention, but you get the picture. They completed seven years of high school between the both of them—crazy as can be!

Richard Williams ~ Father of Tennis Greats

A father who never played tennis before, Richard taught his two little girls how to play the game through what he learned from reading tennis books. He started coaching his little girls in the city of Compton and continued to coach his little girls until they became professional tennis players. His two little girls are women now and have 109 singles titles combined and 28 doubles titles combined. Their combined net worth as of 2019 was around $275 million, and they are known as two of the greatest women tennis players in the history of the game: Venus and Serena Williams. And to think, all of this started with their crazy daddy.

Eric Thomas, PhD ~ From Homeless to PhD

Eric was a high school dropout who ended up homeless, eating out of trash cans. It took him twelve years to earn his undergraduate degree, and he eventually earned his master's degree from Michigan State University in 2005 and his PhD in 2015. He then started doing motivational videos on YouTube and later became one of the most sought-after motivational speakers in the world. He speaks to fortune 500 companies, college teams, NBA teams, NFL teams, high schools, and middle schools. He's also an author of several books, a voice-over personality, a consultant, and a life coach. A homeless high school dropout accomplished all of this. Please get ready to use your Little John voice. *What?!* He was just a crazy homeless guy with crazy dreams, and now he's paid $100,000 or more per speaking engagement.

Robert Nay ~ App Creator

At fourteen, Robert taught himself how to code. He created the game Bubble Ball and put the app online for free with Apple. Over a two-week period, the game would earn him nearly $2 million dollars at the age of fourteen. At the time, he was just a crazy fourteen-year-old kid with a crazy idea. Robert is now a crazy twenty-one-year-old millionaire.

Arnold Schwarzenegger ~ Bodybuilder/Actor/Politician

This crazy kid from Thal Austria, immigrated to America in 1968 and set his sights on being one of the best bodybuilders the world has ever seen. At the age of twenty, he became the youngest person ever to win the Mr. Universe title. He went on to win five Mr. Universe titles and seven Mr. Olympia titles. If that was not crazy enough, after he retired from bodybuilding, he then set his sights on Hollywood to become an actor. Between 1969 and 2017, he starred in thirty-eight films. Some of his most popular films include *The Terminator* franchise, *The Eraser*, *True Lies*, *The Expendables* franchise, *Kindergarten Cop*, *Total Recall*, and *Predator*.

To date, his films have grossed more than $3 billion dollars worldwide. If that isn't crazy enough, he also decided to jump into politics. In 2003, he was voted California's thirty-eighth governor. To top off this crazy roller-coaster ride, he also wrote a book, *Total Recall: My Unbelievably True Life Story*. This kid from Austria came to America and made a life for himself. He is now one of the most recognized and famous human beings on the planet. He's not perfect. He's made his share of mistakes in his personal life, but he was crazy enough to set a goal and stick to it 100 percent.

C. T. Fletcher ~ Bodybuilder

C. T. is known as one of the most intense drug-free powerlifters and bodybuilders on the planet. Although he tried steroids for six months at one point in his career, the price for an extra-hard body started taking a toll on his love life with his wife. He was no longer able to perform in the bedroom, if you know what I mean. As a result, he stopped taking steroids cold turkey. Also, after years of eating unhealthy fast food, he eventually had to have open-heart surgery in 2005 at the age of forty-six. He flat-lined three times on the operating table, but by the grace of God, he made it through. After the surgery, he had to have in-home care. He could barely take care of himself. Family members had to help feed and clothe him during his rehabilitation stage. He's body dwindled down from somewhere in the neighborhood of 225 pounds to 190 pounds, and doctors said he would never be the same.

Instead of feeling sorry for himself, he willed himself back to the gym. Everyone thought he was crazy. It was too much of a risk. They said it was impossible, but he didn't believe it. He came back and won various bodybuilding competitions and went on to become the owner of Iron Addicts Gym where he also sells supplements and clothing merchandise. He has gyms in Signal Hill, California, and Las Vegas Nevada, and plans to open locations in Miami, Florida, and Australia. In 2019, this crazy dude is still going strong at sixty years old.

President Barack Obama ~ 44th President of the United States

Obama served as the forty-fourth president of the United States of America (2008–2016) and was the first African American president in America's history. Half of the world must have thought he was crazy. A black man becoming the president of the United States? Man, please! It had never been done before, so why did he think it could be done? He was just that crazy to think that he could win. With his wife and supporters behind him, he was able to accomplish the unthinkable. A crazy Harvard graduate from Hawaii and the south side of Chicago became the first African American president of the United States of America. Many people around the world never thought there would ever be a black president in the United States of America during their lifetime.

Thomas Edison and Lewis Latimer ~ Inventors

Did you know that Thomas Edison had a thousand failed experiments? He must have been crazy to have a thousand failed experiments and say to himself, "Let's try one more." Because he was crazy enough to move on to 1,001, we now have the light bulb. Isn't it crazy to walk into a dark room, flick a switch, and have the lights come on? Electricity is so crazy! Thank you, Thomas Edison, for the crazy in you. Lewis Latimer, an African American, holds the patents for the electric lamp, issued in 1881, and the patent for the process of manufacturing carbons (the filament used in incandescent light bulbs). He took Edison's invention to an incredible level that changed the world in the way we see it today. He also created the first electric light power station and helped install broad-scale lighting systems for New York, Philadelphia, Montreal, and London. He is the primary reason we can afford electricity and our light bulbs can stay on and function for months and months at a time before we have to change them.

The Three Doctors ~ The Pact

This crazy trio is made up of Dr. Sampson Davis, Dr. Rameck Hunt, and Dr. George Jenkins. They all grew up in New Jersey and first met as students at University High School in Newark, New Jersey. While in high school, these crazy high school students made a pact to get through high school, college, and medical school and go back to their old neighborhood and serve the people there as doctors. They all grew up in neighborhoods notorious for crime and drugs. Three students from the hood made a pact and never wavered. They stuck to their guns, lifted each other up, and never quit until they accomplished the first chapter of their vision. They are now successful doctors, professors, and motivational speakers.

If you want to learn more about these crazy doctors, please pick up one or all three of these books: *The Pact*, *The Bond*, and *We Beat the Street*. You can also order *The Pact*, which is an eighty-four-minute film about their crazy story.

Misty Copeland ~ Ballet Dancer

This crazy little girl from San Pedro California started her ballet studies when she was only 13 years old; which is late in the ballet world. Coming from a family with five siblings and living in a motel, gave her the hunger and drive she needed to pursue her dreams. As she studied and developed her ballet skills, she quickly blossomed into a spectacular dancer with crazy work ethic. She quickly went onto become the first

African American female Principal Dancer with the historic American Ballet Theatre. She was crazy enough to believe she could dance at the highest level despite the odds and open doors for other young ladies that will follow in her footsteps.

- ❖ 2008 ~ Leonore Annenberg (two year) Fellowship
- ❖ 2012 ~ Title Role in "Firebird" (American Ballet Production)
- ❖ 2014 ~ Lead Role in "The Nutcracker" (American Ballet Production)
- ❖ 2014 ~ Lead Role in "Swan Lake" (American Ballet Production)
- ❖ 2014 ~ Appointed by President Obama to the President's Council on Fitness, Sports, and Nutrition
- ❖ 2014 ~ Received Honorary Doctorate from the University of Harford
- ❖ 2015 ~ Lead Role as "Juliet" in Romeo & Juliet (Opera House)
- ❖ Endorsements: American Express, Diet Dr. Pepper, COACH, & Under Armour
- ❖ 2020 ~ Touring ~ Deuce Coupe & Giselle Giselle
- ❖ Books ~ *Your Life in Motion: A Guided Journal for Discovering the Fire in You, Ballerina Body, Life in Motion: An Unlikely Ballerina, Firebird*
- ❖ Film ~ *A Ballerina's Tale*. Producer: Leslie Norville, Misty Copeland biopic, *Life in Motion: An Unlikely Ballerina*. Producer: Nzingha Stewart

Ms. Copeland is not only an inspiration to girls of color, but to all of us. She has relentless work ethic, dedication, and a never quit mentality. She reminds me of a quote of an unknown author which reads, *"Forget her looks. How about her insane work ethic, her unstoppable ambition, and her ridiculously dope soul."*

Mikaila Ulmer, at 11 in 2018 ~ Entrepreneur (www. beessweetlemonade.com)

This young African American entrepreneur was crazy enough to start her own lemonade business. At 10 years old, this crazy little girl had enough courage to go on the popular ABC show "Shark Tank" and was able to strike a deal with investor Daymond John. When she was only 11 years old, she made an $11 million dollar deal with "Whole Food Markets." Now her lemonade is in over 53 stores across the country.

Moziah "Mo" Bridges, at 16 in 2018 ~ Entrepreneur (www. mosbowsmemphis.com)

With help from his grandmother, this crazy young man created his own bow tie business, "Mo's Bows." Daymond John from the popular ABC show, "Shark Tank" is now his mentor. In 2017, with strategic planning and mentoring, he was able to construct a seven-figure deal with the NBA (National Basketball Association). He now has the rights to produce bow ties for all 30 NBA teams. This young man is bold, fearless, and crazy!

If you want to learn more about young and crazy entrepreneurs like Moziah and Mikaila, please visit this youtube link: youtu.be/_ XDI0nIZA68. Black Excellist: 10 Young Black Entrepreneurs & Millennials.

Crazy Is a Good Thing

Correct me if I'm wrong, but it seems like *crazy* is a good thing. Who cares what people think? As long as you believe it can happen and you grind and sweat to make it happen, it will happen. Create a solid support team behind you, and the sky is the limit. Your support team might start off with just books and ideas before you find human beings who can actually see your vision as clearly as you do.

Haters will come and go. I repeat: haters will come and go. They will be the first to tell you that you're crazy. Why are they telling you you're crazy? Number one, they probably don't even know you, and if they do, their perception of your work ethic is likely very low. Number two, they know they are not willing to work that hard to get where you want to go. Number three, it's probably never been done before, and they can't see you making it happen. Number four, it makes no sense to them because they are blind to your vision, your drive, and your obsession.

Only crazy people think they can be the first.

Only crazy people think they can change the world.

Only crazy people think they can make a difference.

Only crazy people compete in marathons and Spartan races.

Only crazy people think they can live in their gift.

Only crazy people live with passion and obsession for what they do.

Only crazy people take risks and give life their all.

Only crazy people think they can be millionaires.

Only crazy people can see themselves living lives no one could ever imagine except for them.

So, let them think you're crazy all day, every day. You will be a better person, and you will learn more and more about yourself at the end of every day. The grind will transform your thought process. You will get beat up every day, and you should expect it. Embrace the pain, and keep moving forward until you can look yourself in the mirror and say, "I have no regrets. I gave it everything I had." Before you go to bed at night, you should get to a point where you can say, "I have no regrets this day." Your thoughts will never be crazy as long as you believe in yourself and your vision.

Crazy people die to live, instead of living to die.

~ Drake

~Notes~

6

_____
_____
_____
_____
_____
_____
_____
_____
_____
_____
_____
_____
_____
_____
_____
_____
_____
_____
_____
_____
_____
_____

I Don't Have Any Time

7

When something becomes important to you, you make the time. We tend to say this when we have lost focus of what's important to us. We tend to say this when we do so much for others that we forget about our own needs. We tend to say this when we have no structure to our days. We tend to say this when we are so wrapped up in our own little worlds that we forget about those closest to us. We tend to say this when we have not yet sat down to think and explore the many possibilities of our true passions and gifts.

There are only twenty-four hours in a day. How do you choose to take advantage of them? Every hour of the day is a gift to enjoy and explore or a gift to throw away. In my opinion, time is the greatest gift that God has ever given us.

The first question we have to ask ourselves is: Why don't I have any time? The next question we need to ask is: Is this thing important enough for me to want to make the time for it? If we decide we want to make the time, the last question we should ask ourselves is: What do I need to do to make the time? What is stopping you from putting in the time and dedication to what is important to you? Who and what is important enough for you to give the gift of your time? Every day that goes by is a day well spent or a day wasted, disappointing and unorganized.

You may need to start waking up at four o'clock in the morning instead of eight o'clock. You may need to start going to the gym in the morning instead of the evening. You may need to start writing that book in the morning. You may need to stay at work and do extra work, so the next day you can leave work an hour early. Free up some time so you can get to your son's or daughter's game. You may need to hire a babysitter once or twice a week, so you can spend some quality time with your significant other. You may need to stop playing video games for four hours at a time and bring it down to an hour. You may need to spend less time on social media, so you can finish your homework or that project. You may need to stop watching so much television and start reading or writing. You simply made need to carve out some more time so you can start spending more time talking with another human being.

We can't let time pass us by and not do what we are capable of doing on any given day. We must continue to use the freedom that we possess to make the most of what we have. I came across a very insightful quote by a golf instructor named Dave Marsh that reads, "We are neither good nor bad. We are free and freedom is everything. True freedom is in your mind to do whatever you believe you're capable of doing!"

Freedom (noun): the state of not being imprisoned or enslaved.

Time (noun): The indefinite continued progress of existence and events that occur in irreversible succession from the past through the present to the future.

365 days = 1 year
12 months = 1 year
30 days = 1 month
168 hours = 7 days
24 hours = 1 day
1,440 minutes = 1 day

We should embrace time and take advantage of it, so it won't take advantage of us. Again, I believe the greatest gift that God has ever given us is time. We need to take care of that gift and stop taking it for granted. I look at life like a game. We only have one game to play, so we need to play at our best when our best is needed. Study the film and play as hard and as passionately as we can, before the clock ticks down to 00:00. The cold thing about the game of life, is that we never know when it's going to end.

True freedom is in your mind, to do whatever
you believe you're capable of doing.

~ Dave Marsh, golf coach

~Notes~

7

_____
_____
_____
_____
_____
_____
_____
_____
_____
_____
_____
_____
_____
_____
_____
_____
_____
_____
_____
_____
_____

It's Too Hard

8

If it were easy, everybody would be doing it. Everybody would have it. Everybody would be rich. Everybody would have that job. Everybody would have that house. Everybody would make the team. Everybody would have the degree he or she wants. Everybody would have that scholarship. I believe the more difficult something is, the more we should embrace it and learn from it. The more we learn, the closer we should get to our goals.

Hard (adjective): Unyielding to pressure and impenetrable or almost impenetrable; difficult to do or accomplish; difficult to control or overcome; involving a great deal of effort.

The harder the task, the harder you should become. Allow the task to shape and mold you into that person who is unyielding to pressure, someone who is not soft but mentally solid and firm. Everything from the way you think to the way you walk to the way you talk should be solid and firm as you move and operate on a daily basis.

If you really want to feel and see what hard looks like, please go down to your local hospital and visit the children's cancer unit. Despite their circumstances, look at the hope on their faces. Please take a visit to your local VA hospital and visit veterans who are in the rehabilitation phase after losing an arm or leg or both. Despite the circumstances, look at the determination in their faces. Please go visit and talk with a man or woman who is paralyzed from the waist or neck down. If you ever get a chance, please find a person who is confined to a wheelchair and see if that individual will share his or her experience with you. That person has no choice but to push through the pain and/or the experience on a daily basis.

Project Wheelchair

When I was working on my undergraduate degree back at the University of Nevada-Reno (1989–1994), I took a health and disabilities class. This class gave me one of the best experiences of my life. I would not trade it for the world. The professor gave us a challenging project we had to complete by the end of the semester. We had to find a partner in class, and we each had to choose a disability and then spend an entire week with our disability out in the community. We also had to find someone who had our disability and interview that person. The goal was to document our experience and report back to the class what we learned from our experience.

The disability that my partner and I chose was being paralyzed from the waist down. We actually had to go and rent a wheelchair for the weekend. The reason I chose this disability was because my grandmother had both of her legs amputated as a young adult. She had to be one of the strongest women I've ever met. I would stay at her house on the weekends growing up. She would cook, she would clean, and she would whip my behind if I got out of line. One night I fell asleep on the couch and woke up the next morning in her bed. What!? Grandma was a superhero!

Let's get back to the project. The wheelchair we rented was a standard wheelchair that you'd see at any hospital. It was an old relic that was harder to operate than I thought. Anyway, we got up early on a Saturday and decided to catch the bus to the mall. So, my partner and I sat at the bus stop early that morning and waited for our bus. When the bus arrived, the bus driver got off of the bus and wheeled me on. He pulled back one of the seats and strapped me in. As we were driving down Virginia Boulevard, we passed up another man who was in a wheelchair waiting for the bus. That's when we realized there was only one wheelchair clamping system per bus. I couldn't help but feel bad that I took his spot on the bus for the purpose of a project.

When we arrived at the mall and started on our journey, I quickly noticed every bump that was on the ground as I wheeled to the mall entrance. When we got inside of the mall, the mall floor was made of tile that sunk down about a half an inch where the grout connected the tiles. That half an inch made for a bumpy ride. I can confidently say, that we able bodied people would never notice that half an inch and how irritating it is. As I wheeled down the mall, I noticed people staring at me, so I decided to play with my facial expressions to see how people would react. If I gave a smile, they generally smiled back. If I had a frown or angry smirk on my face, they would quickly look away.

As we were rolling through the mall, my bladder told me it was time to go to the bathroom. So, we wheeled into the nearest bathroom only to find out that my wheelchair could not fit into any of the stalls. I really had to use the bathroom, so I had my buddy watch the door for me, while I stood up to relieve myself. If I were actually paralyzed from the waist down or didn't have any legs, I most likely would've been forced to pee on myself in that bathroom. We were both disgusted that this was a reality for so many people in wheelchairs, and no accommodations were being made in this mall. I still get upset with myself after all of these years. We should have gone and met with a manager immediately.

My next adventure was simply getting a drink of water from the water faucet. The water faucet was too high for me, so I was unable to reach the water with my mouth. All they had to do was attach a cup dispenser on the wall at a lower level, so patrons in wheelchairs could enjoy a drink of water like everyone else. Again, I'm still kicking myself for not talking to management.

After I left the water faucet, I wheeled over to the shoe department. My partner was close by in another section, observing and taking notes. When I wheeled up, I could see that the shoe salesman was a little uncomfortable. So, of course, I told him I wanted to try on a pair of shoes. I told him my size, and he calmly went to the back to get what I requested.

When he came back, he just placed the shoes on my lap and walked away. I said, "Excuse me! I need to try these on, sir."

He turned around with a puzzled look on his face. He grabbed a shoe out of the box and attempted to put the shoe on my foot. He was so nervous he couldn't even manage to get the shoe on my foot. He asked me,

"Are you sure you wear a size 13?" He was so nervous that he kept trying to force my foot into the shoe without adjusting the laces.

Because he was so nervous, I decided to have a little fun. As he was pounding on the bottom of the shoe, trying to get it on my foot, I decided to scream at the top of my lungs. "Ahhhh!" As soon as I did that, he jumped back and looked as terrified as a black man being pulled over by the police. I looked him in his face and said, "I'm just kidding. I can't feel anything."

My partner was in the other section, trying his best to hold his laughter in. I told the shoe guy to relax and just loosen the laces. He eventually calmed down and managed to get the shoe on my foot. FYI: I did not buy those shoes. His customer service was very poor.

A few days later, we decided to go on campus so we could meet a disabled student we'd set up a meeting with a few days earlier. He was actually paralyzed from the waist down. He was in his early twenties and had been paralyzed since the age of seventeen. He explained to us how he was at a pool party one day. He was having fun with his friends and decided to dive into the pool. As he dove into the pool, a ball was thrown at the same moment. The ball distracted him, he lost focus of the dive, and he hit his head on the bottom of the pool. To share his story with us was truly courageous.

So, moving forward, on the day of the meeting, I just so happen to be walking to campus and a van pulled over next to me. I didn't know who it was until I looked in. It was the guy we were meeting with that day. I was in shock. When I sat down in the van, I was amazed! It was a sweet set up with all hand-operated gears. I had no idea he was capable of driving. I had no idea this was even possible. He was an amazing person who taught me that anything is possible.

The reason for the meeting was so we could interview and videotape him wheeling around campus. What we surprisingly noticed during our video session was that none of the wheelchair lifts on campus were functional. If he had a class in that particular building, he would have to miss class because of his wheelchair. As we were talking in front of one the departments, our courageous tour guide actually had a violent muscle spasm in his lower back while we were filming. He made us feel very comfortable during the process because of his great sense of humor.

While he was having the spasm, he jokingly said, "Hey, you might want to shut the video off. This is not a good look for the ladies." He told us that happens to him periodically. After the spasm, he carried on as if nothing had happened.

We had a great experience talking with him that day about the challenges he faces on a daily basis and how he decides every day to move forward and take care of himself and strive to make a better life for himself, like any other college student.

When I was rolling on campus in my wheelchair, we also noticed there were very few curb cuts on campus. Someone in a wheelchair would literally have to roll his or her wheelchair next to traffic on the roads that went through campus. Instead of just being disgusted and writing a paper about our experience, we actually took our video to the president's office and demanded that the lifts on campus be fixed and the curbs cuts be made. I'm happy to say that one month later, the curb cuts were made and the lifts were operational 24/7, for students in wheelchairs to attend class in those particular buildings.

For one week, I was able to experience firsthand, how hard it is to be confined to a wheelchair. I was also fortunate enough to talk with and experience a college student who was living this life every day and decided each day to make the rest of his life the best of his life. That experience gave me a brand-new perspective on the word *hard*. I can only hope to be half as courageous and brave as our buddy who took time out of his busy life to help us with our project. I wrote the definition of *hard* down for one simple reason—so you could really examine the definition and ask yourself: Will *hard* define my existence, or will I overcome the obstacles and find strength and faith to move forward with my plans and my life every single day? I believe God created us to be more than conquerors and live life abundantly.

Was it too hard for every slave who ever lived? They got up every day from dusk to dawn to make life better for their families, for their slave masters, and for their country. We should never forget how they were whipped, raped, and treated as less than human beings every single day. They had to conquer *hard* and bring him to his knees, so they could live to see the next day. Just that alone should help us all put the word *hard* into a different perspective.

Conquer (verb): To gain, win, or obtain by effort; to gain victory over; to win a war.

Inspirational Movies

I just thought of a few great movies that will inspire you. Sometimes words are just not enough. I tend to be more of a visual learner myself. So, please take some time to rent, buy, or search the internet for at least one of the movies listed. If you've seen them already, watch them again with a different perspective. I guarantee you that any one of these movies will prove to you that *hard* can definitely be brought to its knees.

- *The Pursuit of Happiness*
- *42*
- *The New Edition Story*
- *Rocky I, II, III,* and *IV*
- *Hidden Figures*
- *Hacksaw Ridge*
- *Straight Outta Compton*
- *12 Years a Slave*
- *Remember the Titans*
- *Unbroken*
- *300*
- *Ray*
- *Coach Carter*
- *Queen of Katwe*
- *Lean on Me*
- *The Legend of Bagger Vance*
- *Glory Road*
- *The Bobby Brown Story*
- *Creed*
- *Creed II*
- *The Green Book*
- *The Butler*
- *What's Love Got to Do with It*
- *Django Unchained (A Love Story)*

The harder the task, the harder you should become.

~Notes~

8

The Odds Are Too Great Athletes

9

Everything we want to accomplish in life has a price. The question is, how much are you willing to pay and sacrifice? Will we sacrifice for what we really want? No matter the odds, will we pay the price?

I want to play in the NFL. I want to play major league baseball. I want to play in the NBA/WNBA. I want to play major league soccer. I hear this all the time by so many student athletes, especially those of color. Here are a few questions for you student athletes:

- ❖ Are you willing to get up at three o'clock in the morning and run or go to the gym?
- ❖ Are you willing to shoot two hundred jumpers every day?
- ❖ Are you willing to pass up parties and not drink and smoke?
- ❖ Are you willing to practice every day on your own?
- ❖ Are you willing to watch hours and hours of film?
- ❖ Are you willing to study the game and your position to raise your sport IQ?
- ❖ Are you willing to go to tutoring class?
- ❖ Are you ready and willing to be a leader on and off the court or field?

- ❖ Are you ready and willing to put in the work that no one else is willing to do?
- ❖ Are you ready and willing to be coached? Or do you know it all already?
- ❖ Are you willing to work harder than you've ever worked before after getting cut from the team?

Michael Jordan got cut from his ninth grade basketball team. Did he quit? No. He came back better and stronger the next year. He fought and clawed his way to the top, earning a scholarship to North Carolina. Now, he is considered to be one of the best basketball players who ever lived. He is a NCAA champion. He is a six-time NBA champion and a Hall of Famer! He didn't make it to that level just dreaming and hoping. He worked hard every day of his basketball life to make his dream a reality.

How much are you willing to pay once you know the true numbers? There are roughly 1,086,627 high school football players every year, and only 70,147 NCAA football players. Only 6.5 percent of high school players receive scholarships to college. There are only 256 football players drafted every year (1.5 percent). The number of NFL players who reach year four of their NFL careers is 150.

For those with hoop dreams, here are the numbers: There are roughly 546,000 high school basketball players every year. There are roughly 17,500 college players every year, and there are only forty-eight draftees every year. Out of every 10,000 kids playing basketball in high school, only three will make it to the pros. As of 2014, you must complete one full year of college to be eligible for the NBA draft.

Take a look at these charts, and brace yourself. According to the ncaa. org research team, these charts represent the estimated probability of competing in athletics beyond the high school interscholastic level. The latest update of this information is from April 3, 2019.

Probability Chart (Overall)

Student Athletes	Men's Basketball	Women's Basketball	Football	Baseball	Men's Ice Hockey	Men's Soccer
HS Student Athletes	538,676	433,120	1,086,627	474,791	35,198	410,982
HS Senior Student Athletes	153,907	123,749	310,465	135,6555	10,057	117,423
NCAA Student Athletes	17,984	16,186	70,147	32,450	3,964	23,365
NCAA Freshman Roster Positions	5,138	4,625	20,042	9,271	1,133	6,676
NCAA Senior Student Athletes	3,996	3,597	15,588	7,211	881	5,192
NCAA Student Athletes Drafted	46	32	254	678	7	101
% HS to NCAA	3.3%	3.7%	6.5%	6.8%	11.3%	5.7%
% NCAA to Professional	1.2%	0.9%	1.6%	9.4%	0.8%	1.9%
% HS to Professional	0.03%	0.03%	0.08%	0.50%	0.07%	0.09%

Probability Chart (Men)

Sport	High School Participants	NCAA Participants	Overall % HS to NCAA	% HS to NCAA Division I	% HS to NCAA Division II	% HS to NCAA Division III
Baseball	487,097	35,460	7.3%	2.2%	2.2%	2.9%
Basketball	551,373	18,816	3.4%	1.0%	1.0%	1.4%

Sport	High School Participants	NCAA Participants	Overall % HS to NCAA	% HS to NCAA Division I	% HS to NCAA Division II	% HS to NCAA Division III
Cross-Country	270,095	14,270	5.3%	1.8%	1.4%	2.1%
Football	1,036,842	73,577	7.1%	2.8%	1.8%	2.5%
Golf	114,024	8,609	6.0%	2.0%	1.6%	2.3%
Ice Hockey	35,060	4,229	12.1%	4.8%	0.6%	6.6%
Lacrosse	113,313	14,310	12.6%	3.0%	2.4%	7.2%
Soccer	456,362	25,075	5.5%	1.3%	1.5%	2.7%
Swimming	138,935	9,697	7.0%	2.7%	1.1%	3.2%
Tennis	158,151	7,838	5.0%	1.6%	1.0%	2.3%
Track and Field	600,097	28,698	4.8%	1.9%	1.2%	1.7%
Volleyball	60,976	2,163	3.5%	0.7%	0.6%	2.2%
Water Polo	22,501	1,047	4.7%	2.7%	0.8%	1.2%
Wrestling	245,564	7,239	2.9%	1.0%	0.8%	1.2%

Probability Chart (Women)

Sport	High School Participants	NCAA Participants	Overall % HS to NCAA	% HS to NCAA Division I	% HS to NCAA Division II	% HS to NCAA Division III
Basketball	412,407	16,614	4.0%	1.2%	1.2%	1.6%
Cross-Country	223,518	15,632	7.0%	2.7%	1.7%	2.6%
Field Hockey	59,856	6,103	10.2%	3.0%	1.4%	5.8%
Golf	78,781	5,375	6.8%	2.8%	2.0%	2.1%
Ice Hockey	9,609	2,400	25.0%	8.9%	1.2%	14.9%
Lacrosse	96,904	12,061	12.4%	3.8%	2.7%	6.0%
Soccer	390,482	27,811	7.1%	2.4%	1.9%	2.8%
Softball	367,861	20,316	5.5%	1.7%	1.6%	2.2%
Swimming	175,594	12,848	7.3%	3.3%	1.2%	2.9%
Tennis	190,768	8,068	4.5%	1.5%	1.0%	2.0%
Track and Field	488,592	30,018	6.1%	2.7%	1.5%	1.9%
Volleyball	446,583	17,471	3.9%	1.2%	1.1%	1.6%
Water Polo	21,054	1,216	5.8%	3.6%	1.0%	1.1%

Athletes, listen up. I gave you these numbers because I want you to have the facts for yourself. You will come across a lot of haters on your journeys to greatness. Now they won't be able to tell you anything you don't already know. Some of you will look at these numbers and start to doubt yourself or maybe even quit. Don't do it! If you do, you're cheating yourself and your dream. The odds will always be great. Every professional athlete who has made it to that level couldn't care one red cent about the odds. They had to believe that they were the ones. They had to believe that they were going to die trying to accomplish their ultimate goal of becoming professional athletes.

They had to truly assess their talents and abilities and work from there. No matter how great the odds were, they began the mental and physical grind and never looked back. They began the journey to greatness every day they woke up. This is how we must attack everything we do in life. We have to attack it with relentless fire and enthusiasm. Even if you don't reach your ultimate goal, you still set yourself up with incredible work ethic primed for greatness in whatever you choose to do next.

I'm not just saying all of this because I read it in an article. I lived it! My ninth grade year in junior high, I told myself and my boys that I was going to college for free. I made sure I got up early during the summers and on Saturdays to go to Compton College and run sprints and run the bleachers. I made sure I was in the weight room five days a week. I made sure I never missed a day of practice. As a matter of fact, I started playing organized sports when I was twelve years old, and I never missed a day of practice from the age of twelve through the age of twenty-five. I played football, basketball, and baseball. I made sure that I was not going to be outworked. I made sure that nothing was going to get in the way of my dream.

Playing the Cards That You Are Given

Here are a few playing cards I played with. I was raised by a single mother. We lost her when I was only four years old.

One of my best buddies was shot dead in a drive-by shooting. My other buddy I use to run the streets with was involved in a drive-by shooting and served ten years for that crime. As soon as he got out, his car was sprayed with bullets. He was pronounced dead on arrival.

Statistically, the odds were stacked against me, but I never wavered on my dream of receiving a football scholarship. I even got up at four o'clock in the morning to catch three city buses to get to my high school.

When I was a senior, a rich five-star recruit from Palisades transferred to my school with his own personal quarterback coach. To make a long story short, I had to share time with this other student athlete my last year of eligibility. It was my last and only year to become a starter at the varsity level and show the college scouts what I could do. All of these hurdles made me grind even harder. I will share more about this particular journey in the second half of the book.

By the time my senior season was over, I had helped us win the 1988 California State Championship at Carson High School. Only playing half of the season, I fought my way to earn four recruiting trips. I had the pleasure of visiting Texas A&M, University of Hawaii, Iowa State, and University of Nevada-Reno.

Coach Gatlin's Recruiting Trips

Texas A&M

Let's start with Texas A&M. They had the most beautiful campus and stadium I'd ever seen in my life. The weight room alone appeared to be eighty yards long. I remember guys were able to run the forty-yard dash in the middle of the weight room. If I can remember correctly, they brought in around twenty recruits that weekend to college station. Every recruit was from Texas except for me. After I met the fellas and they learned I was from Compton, my nickname quickly became Eazy for the rest of the weekend. For those who are not familiar with the name Eazy-E, he was a member of the rap group NWA. The life story of the group was made into a movie in 2017 called *Straight Outta Compton*. I look nothing like Eazy-E, but he was one of the most popular members of the group back in 1988.

Let's get back to the recruiting trip. My favorite part of the recruiting trip was when they brought us into the stadium (the twelfth man). We were all standing in the end zone admiring the stadium, and all of a sudden, a voice from the loud speaker started to speak. "Ladies and gentlemen, coming all the way from Compton, California, at six two, 180 pounds. He led the Carson Colts to a 13–1 record. Coming in at quarterback, please welcome *Fred Gatlin*!"

Although the stadium was empty, it felt like it was full of fans. After he called my name, I ran to the fifty-yard line and waved like the stadium was packed with fans. I'm sure that was an amazing experience for all of us. It was definitely an amazing feeling that I will never forget.

After that amazing experience, they walked us into the locker room. As soon as we entered the locker room, we saw our last names on the back of game jerseys hanging in each locker. The jerseys also had our high school numbers on them. When I saw my name on the back of that jersey, I was hooked. I was all in at that moment. They really knew how to sell the dream of playing major college football. I thought this was the place for me.

But unfortunately, I decided not to choose Texas A&M because I was not recruited by this coaching staff. The majority of the coaching staff who recruited me had left the program right before my trip. Jackie Sherrill was the head coach at the time. Once he resigned, a new coaching staff was hired. My trip was already planned and set, so they had to honor it. I was not familiar with any of the coaches when I stepped on campus, but I still had a great time. I guess I was just scared to commit to a school (so far away from home) with a new coaching staff who had not recruited me.

University of Hawaii

My next trip was the University of Hawaii, which was absolutely beautiful. It was really a laid-back environment. The weather was always perfect, and the campus and stadium were really nice. They were 9–3 back in 1988, so they were coming off of a pretty good year with Head Coach Bob Wagner. The coaches were nice guys but a little too laid-back for me. They didn't make me feel like they really wanted me, so I decided to cross them off of my list.

Iowa State

Iowa State was next. The coach from Iowa State started recruiting me during my junior year of high school. He seemed to be a really nice guy, but at the time, my heart told me to trust no one. Anyway, in 1988, when I thought of Iowa, all I could imagine was corn fields, farmers, and a sea of white people. When I was flying in, just about to land, all I saw was fields. I don't know if they were corn fields or not, but in my mind, they sure looked like it.

There are two memories that stick out for me regarding the Iowa State trip. On Friday night, my player hosts took me to the school's auditorium, and to my surprise, they were having a beauty pageant. The beauty pageant was full of African American women. My jaw dropped. I was thinking, *I'm in Iowa. Where did all of these black folks come from?* I believe they were having a Miss Black ISU beauty pageant. This was a great recruiting tactic for a seventeen-year-old kid from Compton. I experienced only one white student in school from elementary school all the way through high school. Anyway, I was pleasantly surprised and had a great time at the pageant.

The second memory that stands out for me is the Saturday night party. I was in my hotel room excited about going to a college party, especially after the beauty pageant. The guys called my room and told me they were on their way to pick me up, so I went down to the lobby to wait. Thirty minutes went by—no big deal. An hour passed by—no big deal. It was ten o'clock at night at this point, and I was thinking the party was just getting started anyway. *It's about to go down*, I thought to myself.

Another hour went by, and now I was starting to get nervous. Remember, there were no cell phones for teenagers back then. So, I actually stayed in the hotel lobby until one o'clock in the morning, waiting. Those fools never showed up! I was pissed! I saw my host the next day and asked him what happened. He said he thought the other guys had picked me up. What? When nobody saw me at the party, I think a bell should have gone off in someone's head. Needless to say, that experience definitely crossed Iowa State off of my list. I told them I was coming, but I just said that so they could hold my scholarship until signing day. I trusted know no one. Especially after my high school experience. Again, more about that experience will come in the second half of the book.

University of Nevada Wolfpack

The University of Nevada was my least exciting trip, but it was my first time seeing snow. The casinos were nice to see as well. One fun moment of the weekend was when they took all of the recruits bowling at Bally's Casino. I believe it's still there today, but they changed the name. It's now called Grand Sierra Resort and Casino. It was a cool trip but nothing too exciting.

When I got back home, I got a call from my future roommate (Wolfpack Hall of Fame wide receiver Treamelle Taylor). Because we were both from the Los Angeles area, the coaches gave him my number to help recruit me because he had already signed his letter of intent from El Camino Junior College. On his recruiting trip, he got a chance to watch their spring game. He not only told me that three quarterbacks had quit, but the starting quarterback was a JC transfer and not very good. That's all I needed to hear. I already knew whichever school I chose to go to, I definitely wanted a chance to play right away. So my choice was an easy one.

So, I chose to attend the University of Nevada-Reno, where I started as a true freshman and earned conference top newcomer of the year and the team offensive MVP. I also earned another offensive MVP trophy my junior year. I won three conference championship rings throughout my college career, and my stats are still in the record books. They're not like the numbers you see today, but they are respectable. I'll also break down more about my stats and some of my college football experiences in the second half.

Professional Mind-Set

After my college career, I went on to play in the CFL (Canadian Football League) with Doug Flutie for the Calgary Stampeders. I also played in Europe for the Milan Rhinos, where I was the starting quarterback. I still have two records in that league. Longest touchdown run from scrimmage (99 yards) and the longest touchdown pass from scrimmage (95 yards). You can check out the highlights on YouTube. Just type in "Fred Gatlin QB."

The only reason I did not play in the NFL is because my mind-set and my grind was not at a championship level. My mind-set was at a playoff level. I worked hard enough to be good but not great. I didn't study the game at a championship level. I didn't study film at a championship level. I didn't study my quarterback position at a championship level. I let outside noise clutter my mind. My grind was not strong enough. My mind was not strong enough to endure the years of pain and suffering it takes to get to the top of the highest mountain.

When I look back, I have no one to blame but myself. I was good, but I was not great. The experience was great, but the path could have been different if I would've had a slightly different mind-set. Canada and Europe were not bad, but we all know the NFL is the ultimate destination for little boys who dream of playing professional football.

Aspiring professionals: Don't do what I did. Do better! The odds were stacked against me, and I made it to a certain level. The odds did not stop me from chasing my ultimate goal of playing in the NFL; my mind-set stopped me. The real odds that you have to overcome are the odds in your own mind. You must be relentless in your physical and mental grind. You must be relentless in your quest for new information and the right information. You must be relentless in your fight against ignorance. You must be relentless in your grind for mental and spiritual growth. You must be relentless in keeping yourself around other champions. You want to be around peers and mentors you can learn from. You want to surround yourself with people who push you on those days when you stop pushing yourself.

Relentless (adjective): Unyielding, strict or harsh; unrelenting, never stopping an attack.

Ignorance (noun): Lack of knowledge.

Grind (verb): To work or study laboriously (requiring much work, exertion or perseverance); to reduce to fine particles, as by pounding or crushing. (Greatness is in the details.)

Perseverance (noun): Steady persistence in a course of action, a state, etc., especially in spite of difficulties, obstacles, or discouragement.

Champion (noun): A person who has defeated all opponents in a competition or series of competitions; a person who fights for or defends any person or cause; a person who wins, despite the odds against him or her.

I constantly repeat this next quote to my students and my athletes; "You must be allergic to average! Good is not good enough! Greatness is the ultimate goal!" The difference between an average person and a person who is striving to be great every day is an inch.

In football, you can win or lose a game by an extra point. In basketball, you can win or lose a game by one point at the buzzer. In school, you could be one assignment away from an A. In college, you can be one class or one semester away from getting that degree that will help change your financial situation forever. In golf, one made putt could be the difference between a win and a loss or the difference in millions for professional golfers. In business, you could be one talking point away from getting that contract. Olympians work hard for years and years to be great for just a few seconds or minutes on the biggest stage in the world. They understand that the inch they've been working for all of their lives will potentially change their lives forever. Those who strive to be great work hours and hours for that one inch. Consistently paying attention to details is a must. Knowing and doing the little extras that others are not willing to do will set you apart from the pack.

The inches we need are everywhere around us, they're in every break of the game, every minute every second! We claw with our fingernails for that inch; because we know, when we add up all of those inches, that's going to make the difference between winning and losing, between living and dying! In any fight, it's the guy who's willing to die, who's going to win that inch!
~ Al Pacino, Any Given Sunday

The Dream is Free but the Hustle is sold separately!
~ George "GK" Koufalis

Athletes Know it All

10

Fourteen Tips for the High Profile Athlete

1. If what you do comes extra easy for you, don't let that be your curse. Don't let your talent cause you to be lazy and have below-average work ethic. The young man or lady who has less talent will surpass you. If the other person's work ethic is superior to yours, you will be left behind because that person's hunger is greater than yours. That person will take your scholarship, your starting position, or your spot on that professional team in the future. If you take at least one page out of the book of Michael Jordan (Bulls), Kobe Bryant (Lakers), Cristiano Ronaldo (Juventus FC), Jake Diekman (Texas Rangers), Stephen Curry (Warriors), LeBron James, (Cavs, Heat, Lakers), Tiger Woods (PGA), Tom Brady (Patriots), or Shaun White (snowboarder), your future will be unlimited. All of these individuals are world champions and work harder or have worked harder at their crafts than anyone on the planet. If you don't work harder than your teammates, opponents, or haters, you don't deserve anything.

2. Eat a good breakfast every day. Start your day with the proper nutrients you need, so your mind and body will have an advantage before the day starts.

3. Learn from the mistakes of others. The signs are always there. Open your eyes and see what's going on around you. Listen to wise people who are giving you sound advice.

4. Pick your friends wisely. Whoever you hang around with the most will influence you the most. Are your friends helping you reach your goals, or are they pushing you away from them? You have everything to lose. Stay away from risky parties. Stay away from fights. Stay away from drugs and alcohol. Research shows that most alcoholics and drug addicts took that first drink or first hit between the ages of fifteen and seventeen.

5. Read! Expand your mind-set on a daily basis. Read something every day. Read something that jolts your imagination. Find articles about the schools you want to go to. Find articles about the recruiting process. You have reading material at your fingertips every day. Your phone can be a blessing or a curse. You can read one sentence, one paragraph, or a couple of chapters. Just read! Listen to an audio book or motivational speech if you have to. If your mind is not growing and changing on a daily basis, the only thing it can undoubtedly do is slowly die.

6. Watch and study the film. Study the film of yourself and your opponents. Study the game and raise your sport IQ to the highest level possible. Try your best to become the smartest player on the field. Study and watch film so much that you begin to know the game plan better than the coach.

7. Clean up your social media pages. If there is anything on those pages you cannot show your mother, father, or grandmother, delete it. College recruiters try their best to find out as much as they can about you before they make an investment.

8. Update your highlight reel. You only need four or five good plays. Scouts do not have time to watch a ten-minute video. You have to slap them hard with your best stuff. Get their attention in the first few seconds they start watching. If you make better plays in the future, you may want to go back and evaluate what you have up. Make changes as needed.

9. Don't let the opposite sex distract you from your goals. Risky behavior can jeopardize and detour your future in ways that you

could definitely imagine. You know who she is. You know who he is. You know who they are. Think about it. Is that person toxic? Is your behavior toxic to your future? If you don't know, you better ask somebody.

10. Keep your mind open to all of the possibilities out there. Division I, Division II, Division III, NAIA, and colleges in Canada or even Europe. Don't let your pride stop you from doing what you need to do even if it's at a smaller college. You may even look into junior colleges that give two-year scholarships in certain parts of the country. Not only do they give scholarships, but many of them have dorms on campus as well.

11. Don't let the odds scare you. Change your mind-set. If you fight and grind as hard as you can, the odds will start tipping in your favor. The odds are that positive things will happen for you if you exhaust all of the possibilities of going to college. You will find that college, or that college will find you.

12. Study, study, study! Make sure you are getting the best grades you can possibly get. Take the SAT or ACT practice test before you take the real tests. Make sure you talk with your counselors. Make sure you are taking all of the required high school classes, so you will be eligible to attend the multitude of colleges that are out there.

13. If you are given a red shirt year, use it and use that college to pay for your master's degree in five years. Take extra classes every summer to get this done.

14. Find and print out Coach John Wooden's Pyramid of Success poster.

Watch, listen and learn. You can't know it all yourself.
Anyone who thinks they do is destined for mediocrity.
~ Author Unknown

~Notes~
10

_____
_____
_____
_____
_____
_____
_____
_____
_____
_____
_____
_____
_____
_____
_____
_____
_____
_____
_____
_____
_____
_____

The System Is Not Designed for Me African American Golf Legends

11

I was doing some research and found some great articles by BlackEnterprise. com and the African American Registry (aaregistry.org). I also purchased a book, *Uneven Lies* by Pete McDaniel, Which is an excellent book. During my research, I was able to find a multitude of African American professional golfers whom many people have never heard of. These golfers had it hard in their perspective journeys in life but found a way to persevere through the pain and suffering of prejudice and racism. They teach us how to never give in and never give up.

If you get a free moment, please take the time to research some of these players. You'll be amazed by their individual stories. They were obsessed with their passion to play golf at the highest level in our country, where playing golf while black made a lot of people embrace their emotions of anger, nervousness, hatred, and fear, which ultimately created many acts of discrimination and racism. Despite all of the physical, mental, and emotional obstacles that were placed in front of these men and women, they managed to persevere and grind their way to the top of their game and to the top of humanity. These men and women helped change the way a lot of Americans viewed black players and black people in general during those challenging times in American history. The individual journeys of the following golfers really move and inspire me for many different reasons.

Teddy Rhodes (1913–1969)

Born in 1913 in Nashville, Tennessee, Rhodes grew up during segregated times in the South. He taught himself how to play using an old number two iron. He would practice many days and nights at the city park. As his game grew and he started to master several parts of his game, he caught the attention of golf-crazed heavyweight champ Joe Louis in 1946. In exchange for golf instruction, Joe Louis would sponsor Rhodes to play in many golf tournaments. He won 150 times on the all-black UGA tour (United Golf Association). Despite the Caucasian-only rule that the PGA had adopted, he fought his way to play in the 1948 US Open at the Riviera Country Club in Los Angeles. He shot a seventy in the first round but faded to the back of the pack during later rounds, eventually losing to one of the greatest ball strikers to ever play the game, Ben Hogan. In the 1960s, Rhodes mentored several black PGA players, including Charlie Sifford and Lee Elder. In 1998, Rhodes was inducted into the Tennessee Golf Hall of Fame.

Lee Elders (1934–)

He is best remembered for becoming the first African American to play in the Masters Tournament in 1975. In 1979, he became the first African American to qualify to play in the Ryder Cup. He taught himself to play golf by sneaking onto all-white courses at night. He never actually played a round of golf until he was sixteen years old. After being discharged from the US Army in 1961, he joined the UGA and won five national championships. In one stretch of tournaments, he amazingly won twenty-one of twenty-three golf tournaments. In 1967, he became one of the first black golfers on the PGA tour. In 1968 he battled with Jack Nicklaus in the American Golf Classic. Nicklaus finally won the tiebreaker and the tournament with a birdie after four grueling holes. Elder and his wife created a scholarship fund in 1974 to offer monetary aid to low-income young men and women seeking money for college.

Charlie Sifford (1922–2015)

He earned sixty cents a day as a caddie at the Carolina Country Club. He would use that money to help his mom keep the household together financially. A former pro by the name of Sutton Alexander took an interest in Sifford and took him under his wing. By the age of thirteen, he was shooting par. By the time he was seventeen years old, the country club members really started to take notice. Alexander had to pull Sifford aside one day and tell him that his caddie services were no longer needed. He felt it best that he stay away from the country club. The reason for this sudden change was for Sifford's own safety. The country club members did not like the fact that he had become so good. They simply did not want him on the course embarrassing members with his consistent game and consistent ball striking, so he had to go.

In the 1950s, he dominated the Negro National Open, capturing the title six times. He was often counseled by Jackie Robinson, who was the first African American to break into the major leagues. In 1957, Sifford was the first African American golfer to beat red, white, and blue players in a PGA cosponsored tournament by winning the Long Beach Open. In 1991, his career earnings had grown to $1.2 million. This was definitely a huge jump from the sixty cents a day he made as a caddie. He played in 422 PGA tournaments, and in 2004, he was inducted into the World Golf Hall of Fame. He endured racism and exclusion from numerous PGA events and still beat the odds.

Calvin Peete (1943–2015)

This man did not start playing golf until he was twenty-three years old. He taught himself how to play by reading books and watching videos of his swing. It took him nine years to create a solid golf game where he was consistently shooting under par. He turned pro at the age of thirty-two. He was a high school dropout with a crooked left arm due to a broken bone that never healed correctly after he fell out of a tree. Despite his crooked arm, he was one of the PGA's most accurate drivers off the tee, as well as a great fairway-to-green player. At one point, he won the Driving Accuracy Award on tour five years in a row. From 1976 to 1995, he played in 344 tournaments and won twelve times on the PGA tour. His best finish in the Masters was eleventh place. He was also on two Ryder Cup teams with Jack Nicklaus, Tom Watson, Ben Crenshaw, Curtis Strange, and other stars who helped the United States triumph over the European team.

Althea Gibson (1927–2003)

This woman was simply amazing. She was a two-sport athlete. According to biography.com, Gibson was the first African American tennis player to compete at the US National Championships in 1950 and the first African American player to compete at Wimbledon in 1951. She won the women's singles and doubles at Wimbledon in 1957 and won the US Open in 1958. In one stretch from 1947 to 1956, she won ten straight championships. Not only did she break racial barriers in women's tennis, but she broke down walls in women's professional golf as well. Before Serena and Venus Williams, there was Althea Gibson. She was the first black woman to ever compete on the women's pro tour in golf.

Bill Spiller (1913–1988)

He did not take up the game of golf until he was thirty years old. He created his swing based off of the many swings of his favorite PGA tour stars. By the mid-1940s, he had won several black amateur tournaments in Southern California. As a pro, he played in the UGA (United Golfers Association). In 1948 he shot a sixty-eight to tie Ben Hogan for second place after the first round of the Los Angeles Open at the Rivera Country Club. He eventually lost to Hogan, but his finish made him eligible to play in the Richmond Open the next week. When he showed up for the tournament, the PGA tour officials turned him away by enforcing the Caucasian-only clause. Regardless of many setbacks in his career and life, Spiller was relentless with his obsession to play on the PGA tour so he could make a living like his white counterparts. He was a pillar of change for so many. He, along with others, forced the PGA to look at their rules concerning African American golfers and eventually forced change and acceptance.

Jim Thorpe (1949 –)

He finished first on the Champions Tour thirteen times. Over his long career, he's beaten some of the greats in the likes of Jack Nicklaus, Tom Watson, and Fred Funk. He also won on the PGA tour three times. He now serves as ambassador to Tobago's Junior Golf Academy in Trinidad.

Pete Brown (1935–2015)

He not only had the challenge of dealing with segregation during his career, he also had to overcome polio to become a professional golfer. He won on the UGA tour four times. He played on the PGA tour for seventeen years. He won twice on the PGA tour and was the first African American to ever win a tournament on tour (1964 Waco Turner Open). He posted fourteen professional wins in his long career.

Tiger Woods (1979 –)

If you asked many golf fans around the world, they would probably say that Tiger Woods is the greatest golfer who ever played the game. He is the first African American to win the Masters. He has eighty-two PGA tour wins, which is tied for the most wins in PGA history. He's won the Masters five times, the US Open three times, the Open Championship three times, and the PGA Championship four times. Which means he has fifteen major championships under his belt. His peers say he is one of the most mentally strong golfer's they've ever played against. Tiger Woods took the golf world by storm by demonstrating tireless work ethic, practicing hours upon hours on the range and on the greens, studying film, hitting the weights, and going through backbreaking Navy Seal training.

He has set the blueprint for many young golfers today, regarding how much work has to be done to play at the highest level week in and week out. Not many golfers were lifting weights before Tiger Woods came along. Tiger Woods has single-handedly put the PGA tour on his back. He is one of the sole reasons for the recent popularity of the sport by non-golf fans around the world and the lucrative payouts that his peers enjoy on tour. He is currently designing golf courses all around the world, and his Tiger Woods Foundation is helping thousands upon thousands of students develop their college and career-ready skills. His estimated net worth as of 2018 was $750 million.

After a public divorce, infidelity, and mental anguish. Tiger came back to win five more tournaments before injuries forced him to take a two-year layoff from the game. During his layoff, he was able to reestablish a great friendship with his ex-wife and strengthen the bond he has with his two kids. After five long winless years, he finally got his eightieth win on tour, winning the 2018 PGA Tour Championship. His doubters who said he would never win again on the PGA tour were silenced on that day.

Many said he would never win another major. But, on April 14, 2019, he proved his naysayers wrong. He won one of the biggest golf tournaments in the world: The Masters Championship. This is the Super Bowl of golf. He won his eighty-first PGA tournament, as well as his fifth green jacket and fifteenth major. On October 27, 2019, he played in the Zozo Championship in Tokyo, Japan, and won his eighty-second PGA golf title. He is now tied for the most wins in PGA history.

Regarding majors, he is now only three away from tying the great Jack Nicklaus, who holds the record for most major victories in golf history, with eighteen. Tiger Woods's career statistics alone are just mind-boggling. For anyone to doubt him is ridiculous to me.

He had to overcome huge mountains to get his life and game back on track. We're talking about multiple back surgeries and not being able to swing a golf club or walk for a long period of time. The man was out of the game for almost two years with a public scandal hovering over his head, along with a public divorce. At one point, he even doubted if he would ever play competitive golf again. He fought and fought and fought his way back to being one of the best golfers in the world once again. Coming back after all that had happened to him privately and in the public eye is simply amazing. This was and still is probably one of the greatest comebacks, in sports history.

Thankfully, there were great men who came before him. They not only opened doors for him to walk through; they allowed him the opportunity to kick those doors off the hinges. With the guidance of his late father Earl Woods, Tiger Woods has been able to excel and bounce back at different stages of his career and his life. Even in his darkest hours, he has been able to push through and see the light at the other end. You can either love him or hate him. The choice is yours. But you can't deny what he has accomplished thus far in his exceptional career. You can't deny that he appreciates the game more, and he has become a better man because of his mistakes and life lessons. In my opinion, he is the best to ever play the game. His best is still yet to come.

Ben Hogan (1912–1997)

Ben Hogan is not an African American golfer, but he is considered one of the best ball strikers the game has ever seen. He won sixty-four times on tour, including nine majors. He is now in the World Golf Hall of Fame. He also taught me some very fundamental aspects of the golf swing in his book *Five Lessons*, which have become the foundation of my swing.

Like many men across the country, Hogan did not have a father in his life. It is believed that he witnessed his father commit suicide. His father shot himself in the head right in front of him. After this horrific event, he was still able to mentally function and create a life and career for himself. At the age of nine, he had to go to work after school as a paperboy and later on as a caddie, to help with the household finances. After many years and multiple wins on the PGA tour, he was involved in a terrible car accident in 1949. This car accident almost ended his career.

Sixteen months after that crash, he returned to the tour and won the 1950 US Open. He magically won that tournament by playing thirty-six holes on the final day of competition. He was always determined to win, no matter what. The odds were stacked against him, but he came out on top every time. He is a legend in the golf world. As I did my research, his story was just too compelling for me to leave out.

Honorable Mention ~ George Franklin Grant (1846–1910)

He was a dentist and a professor at Harvard University. He was credited by the USGA (United States Golf Association) as the inventor of the modern tee (1899). The golf tee is used today in every golf round known to man. For those who don't play golf, a tee is a wooden peg that is inserted into the ground. For the first shot of every hole, the golfer has an option to place the ball on top of the peg (which balances the ball inches from the ground) before swinging at it with his/her club.

Competition Against the Odds

No one can deny that African American golfers overcame huge obstacles in the game of golf. They were pillars and examples for the way black players were perceived on and off the course. They broke down barriers and roadblocks and gave masses of people hope and a greater perspective of the power of the human spirit. They looked at the overall picture, grabbed a pen, and drew themselves in—permanently.

Every day is a competition against the odds. Compete today, young man. Compete today, young lady. Compete today, Mom. Compete today, Dad. Compete today! Don't let the numbers define your willingness to work. Will you be average today, or will you stay on the grind and be a champion today? We must revisit our goals on a daily basis and give them life, or they will slowly die with us. Champions have paved the road for other champions to follow in their footsteps and do even greater things than they could ever imagine. Rise, champion. The system was designed for you. Some people just don't know it yet.

Every day is a competition against the odds!

~Notes~

11

_____
_____
_____
_____
_____
_____
_____
_____
_____
_____
_____
_____
_____
_____
_____
_____
_____
_____
_____
_____
_____
_____
_____
_____
_____

It's Too Expensive

12

Expensive (adjective): Very high-priced; costly.

Your life is priceless. Nothing should be too expensive for you. You deserve the best. I'm reminded on a daily basis that we all have to pay an astronomical amount of sweat equity, pride, embarrassment, doubt, failure, and money if we want to acquire the things that we want and need for ourselves and others.

Here are a few questions that only you can answer for yourself. These same questions will continue to show their face throughout this entire book.

1. Does it cost too much to wake up every morning at two o'clock in the morning, so you can write that book you've been wanting to write?
2. Does it cost too much to take out a school loan so you can go back to school, get that degree, and make the money you deserve?
3. Does it cost too much to shoot two hundred extra jumpers, swim ten more laps, hit two more buckets of balls, catch fifty more passes, or hit one hundred more balls in the batting cage after practice, so you can help your team win, earn a scholarship, or make it to the pros?

4. Does it cost too much to leave work early, so you can go attend your son/daughter's game, performance, or academic competition?
5. Does it cost too much to stay up until three o'clock in the morning, so you can finish that project that will get you that A in class or get you that contract you need?
6. Does it cost too much to say hello and start a conversation with someone who may be depressed?
7. Does it cost too much to go to counseling or therapy to help save your sanity?
8. Does it cost too much to pay for a seminar that will help start or save your business?
9. Does it cost too much to attend acting, piano, dance, or singing lessons after school or after a long day of work to follow your dreams and allow your gift to blossom?
10. Does it cost too much to go to the gym at four o'clock in the morning or six o'clock in the evening before or after a long day at school, practice, or work to improve your health or improve your strength, so you can be the best you can be on and off the playing field of life?
11. Does it cost too much to pray and meditate for a few minutes every day on positive affirmations?

Degree or Bust

In 1994, I had one semester (eighteen credits) of school left to earn my bachelor's degree. My scholarship eligibility was over, so I had to pay for the semester out of pocket. The cost of tuition for the semester at the time was around five thousand dollars with books included.

I was living back in Compton with my parents (my aunt and uncle) at the time. My professional football career had not taken off like I imagined it would. My first season in the CFL was over, and I only made $500 per week on the practice squad. Once I got back home, I only had a few months before the beginning of the semester was going to start. So, I had to quickly have a brief conversation with myself. I told myself, "If I don't go back to school now, I'll never go back." A few months earlier, I had sold my 1985 Pontiac Fierro for $1,600. When I came to the revelation that I needed to go back to school, I only had $600 to my name. If I was going to go back to school, I needed to pay for tuition, books, rent, food, and a plane ticket to Reno.

One of my family members told me I might as well forget it. "You don't have the money to pay for all that." Again, I whispered to myself and said, "If I don't go back now, I'll never go back. I have to find a way. I'm out!" So, I called my old college roommate who I knew was moving back to Reno and asked him if I could stay with him. When he said yes, I knew I had to go. My main man, my trusted wide receiver and University of Nevada Hall of Famer Treamelle Taylor, came through in the clutch once again.

So, I went ahead and bought my one-way plane ticket to Reno, not knowing how I was going to pay for tuition, books, rent, and food for the next five months. I just knew I had to make a move. A few days later, I was on a plane headed to Reno, Nevada, with about $450 in one pocket and determination and faith in the other. I knew no matter what, I was not going to leave Reno without my degree.

The entire flight up to Reno, I was trying to figure out a plan in my head. I had $450 to my name, and I had to plan out a strategy of how I was going to afford to go to school, pay rent, and eat for the next five months. As soon as I touched down and stepped off of that plane, reality hit me quickly. I had to think quickly because the semester would be starting in three weeks.

The first thing I did was call my boy to confirm that I still had a place to stay. When I got to the apartment, I told him that I would have my portion of the rent every month. I had too much pride to let him know I only had $450 to my name.

I knew I had to make some decisions very quickly if I was going to make all of this work. My faith in God and my determination to succeed was all I had on my side. So, I slept on it and woke up the next morning with a plan. I got dressed and went straight to campus to look for my old team doctor. During my years of playing for the Wolfpack, he used to always say, "If you ever need anything, don't hesitate to ask." Those words hit me early that morning, so I went to go see what "if you ever need anything" really meant.

I walked into his office and told him why I was back in town. I basically said, "This is my last semester in school, and I am not leaving this town until I graduate. When I played here, you said if I ever needed anything, don't hesitate to ask."

He said without pause, "No problem."

Just like that, my tuition was paid. The Bible does say, "Ask and you shall receive. Seek and you shall find. Knock and the doors shall be opened" (Mattthew7:7; NIV Version). One hurdle down and it was on to the next one. Next, I needed to get my books paid for.

The next day I went to go see a professor who was also one of my mentors, who was also running a community outreach program. I told him my plans for the semester, and he gave me an opportunity. He said if I volunteered to mentor a high school student for the semester, the program would pay for all of my books. Just like that, in the span of two days, tuition and books were paid for.

The final hurdle was paying my portion of the rent every month and eating every day. I had to humble myself and go get a job as a pizza delivery guy. Coach Len Stevens, a retired University of Nevada head basketball coach, gave me a job. He was the owner of the pizza joint. I remember going to people's doors and hearing, "Hey, aren't you the Gatlin Gun? Hey, Mom, it's Gatlin, he's delivering our pizza."

See, in Reno, the college football team was and still is the biggest show in town. Needless to say, I was very popular when I played. I used to sign hundreds of autographs after games and do several interviews. In my mind, I was supposed to go the NFL, but I wasn't drafted. My mind was not prepared, and I was not invited to any NFL training camps. So, here I was, after one year in the CFL, delivering pizzas to survive.

I made just enough money to feed myself and pay my portion of the rent sometimes. Some months, I just did not have it. One month, I had to call a buddy of mine who was playing in the NFL at the time. A year earlier, he told me if I ever needed anything, don't hesitate to call. I remembered what he said, so I decided to take him up on his offer as well. So, as hard as it was, I broke my ego down, and I called him up and asked for $500. Within thirty minutes, he was at my front door with $500 cash—no judgement, no questions asked. He just delivered for me. I can never forget Henry Rolling. He played for Tampa Bay, the San Diego Chargers, and the Los Angeles Rams. He's also in the University of Nevada Hall of Fame and is a great guy!

So, I was able to pay my portion of the rent for the next two months. Fortunately for me, back in 1994 a halfway decent two-bedroom apartment in Reno, Nevada was going for $450 a month. My roommate also came through for me as well. When I came up short on the rent a few times, my boy Treamelle covered the cost with no questions asked. God's favor, faith, and determination lead the way for me the entire time.

I share this particular story because if I had not made the decision to go back to school, I don't know what type of life I would be living today. I definitely would not have a twenty-four-year career in education and be the Principal of my own school.

When it was all said and done, in May 1994, I was able to complete eighteen credits and walk across the stage to receive my bachelor's degree. Getting my bachelor's degree was a great springboard that launched me toward my master's degree. I received my master of arts from Pepperdine University in 1998 and my administrative credential, which is equivalent to a second master's degree, from Bradman University.

In my opinion, the real reward of paying the cost, is not in the result but in the process. What we go through to get to the result is where the real riches are. The journey we take in our quest for change, for happiness, and for greatness is the key that opens every door that we need. The journey is what shapes and molds us. The journey strengthens us. The journey changes us. The journey shows us what we are capable of enduring. The journey teaches us things about ourselves that we never knew we had inside of us. The journey teaches us about the survival of the fittest. Are you willing to hunt for greatness when it's dark and you can't see what's ahead of you, or will you run like a coward because you're scared of the dark and the unknown?

I'm in hell's kitchen with an apron and a hair net.
- Lil Wayne

~Notes~

12

_____
_____
_____
_____
_____
_____
_____
_____
_____
_____
_____
_____
_____
_____
_____
_____
_____
_____
_____
_____
_____
_____
_____

They Don't Believe in Me

13

Who cares! The only person who needs to believe in you is you. When others see your obsession with yourself and your vision, they have no choice but to say you're crazy and you're not going to make it!

Believe (verb): To have confidence in the truth, the existence, or the reliability of something, although without absolute proof that one is right in doing so.

King of Comedy

I don't think too many people believed in Steve Harvey when he was homeless and living in his car. According to Harvey, he was making as little as fifty dollars a week. He had to wash up in gas stations and hotel bathrooms as he chased his dream of being on television as a comedian. He worked his way through homelessness, divorce, and a $20 million dollar tax lien. He leaned heavily on God, faith, tireless work ethic, belief in himself, professionalism, a never-quit attitude, and his inner circle who believed in him. That was the only way he would be able to walk through the fire and come out on the other end.

Now, he is a living example of perseverance, hard work, discipline, and wisdom. He is living in his gift, and his gift has opened other doors for his gift to shine. He has done countless stand-up acts all across the country. He was part of the successful comedic tour Kings of Comedy. He did one hundred episodes of *The Steve Harvey Show*. He has a syndicated radio talk show and he hosts one of the most popular game shows in the world, *Family Fued*. He has written several books, some of which have adapted to the big screen. He's a motivational speaker and also runs mentoring camps for boys all across the nation. His net worth is estimated at $100 million. In my opinion, his net worth is priceless.

Whether you agree or disagree with his politics, his past mistakes, his philosophy about dating, his philosophy on business, or even his meeting with Donald Trump, you have to give him respect for digging and clawing his way from doubt and despair to where he is now. He's in the category of a select few who have been invited to sit down and talk not only with President Trump but with President Obama as well. How many people from his humble beginnings can say that? He is now able to provide for his family and countless others. God has elevated him to high levels of influence all across the world.

Perseverance (noun): Steady persistence in a course of action, a purpose, a state, etc., especially in spite of difficulties, obstacles, or discouragement.

Discipline (noun): Activity, exercise, or a regimen that develops or improves a skill; training; the rigor or training effect of experience, adversity, etc.; staying committed or focused.

Wisdom (noun): The quality or state of being wise; acting in a positive or logical manner or making quality decisions according to information that has been retrieved or retained.

For many of us, our friends may not believe in us. Our teachers may not believe in us. Our coworkers may not believe in us. Our own parents may not even believe in our dreams. It doesn't matter. You have to believe in yourself. You have to grind and surround yourself with people who can charge your battery when needed. You can learn something from them, and hopefully, they can learn something from you. When it's dark and you can't see anything in front of you, you must continue to take steps forward. Put your arms out in front of you, and feel your way around until you can feel the light switch. When you feel it, you'll know it. When the light switch is turned on, you'll be amazed at what you see and how far you've gone and how much farther you can go.

Believe in God and believe in yourself. He will send you everything else you need to persevere through the pain and suffering that you will go through before victory is ultimately accomplished.

Faith: Believe those things that are not as though they were.

The only person that needs to believe in you, is you! Work like you're broke!
~ Tyler Perry

~Notes~

13

School Is a Waste of Time

14

Formal schooling is the foundation of every footstep we make toward a better tomorrow, which should be filled with hope, purpose, and financial freedom. Traditional school should teaches us how to socialize with our peers, deal with difficult peer groups, engage in group/team activities, and conduct ourselves and operate in the culture in which we find ourselves every day. It also should teach us the fundamentals of reading, writing, multiplying, adding, subtracting, and financial literacy. I believe formal schooling should be a mirror of what's going on in our society.

The Mirror

You have the high achievers and the low achievers. You have sports stars and fans. You have elected officials and the common body. You have parents and students fighting for their rights. You have peer pressure pushing you to do the right thing or the wrong thing. There are people who are bullied. There are people who see others bullied and do nothing to stop it. There are also those who've been bullied and have triumphed over those horrible situations. You have teachers and coaches you love and those you hate. You have administrators who lead with compassion and understanding and others who are micromanagers and lead with a dictatorship mentality. There's a strong culture on every campus. People grow within the culture and find pieces of their identities with each group, club, activity, or team they are associated with.

All of these situations are reflections of what we see and experience at home, at work, in our relationships, and in the many activities we participate in, on and off campus. We must be aware and learn how to take advantage of the many lessons (good and bad) that are taught every day in public and private schools.

The quality of teaching may not be great in some places, but the experience is priceless. When you do find a great teacher or program, you must take advantage of the opportunity and store away as much information as possible.

Day School

I don't view school as just being in a building. In my opinion, school is in session each and every minute of the day. School is in session where ever we go. The lessons come from many places like church, the barber shop, mama's kitchen, family reunions, team sports, the neighborhood, that first breakup, that butt whuppen, that punishment, prom night, that house or car purchase, or maybe even that movie we just saw. There's always something new to learn about ourselves, our surroundings, our parents, our kids, our jobs, our friends, our boyfriends or girlfriends, our spouses, our history, our financial literacy, our love, and the list goes on and on. We should try to learn something new about ourselves and life every day. With growth, there's definitely change.

As long as we are alive, school will always be in session. The idea of school can never be a waste of time. It can only be a waste of opportunities to learn something about something and apply that something to your life. There are a lot of people in our society who have limited formal education but yet make six figures, while others are millionaires. These people have tremendous work ethic and have heavily educated themselves in their fields of expertise. So in my opinion, school can never be a waste of time. As soon as we open our eyes every morning, school is in session.

Look in the mirror and see what you need to
see and learn from every experience.

~Notes~
14

_____
_____
_____
_____
_____
_____
_____
_____
_____
_____
_____
_____
_____
_____
_____
_____
_____
_____
_____
_____
_____
_____

I Need More Sleep

15

I quoted Dr. Thomas earlier when I wrote, "Sleep is the new broke!" This is actually one of my favorite quotes. You know, some of us literally lie in the bed too long and waste too much of our day away, while others are consciously up and moving but yet still sleepwalking on the treadmill of life. Sleep literally means there is a lack of consciousness. We need rest; we don't need sleep. Rest is when you shut the body down to recharge for the next opportunity to learn. You recharge for the next idea to move you into action. You recharge for the next opportunity to wake up and grind. The harder we grind, the harder we can play when it's time to play. In my opinion, sleep is when you are wasting valuable time and not even conscious of it.

The National Sleep Foundation suggest that we need between seven and nine hours of rest every day for our overall health and well-being. I can respect that. It makes all the sense in the world. Well, there are only two options if you want to be more productive and get more done throughout the course of a day.

Option 1

Go to bed earlier. For example, if you go to bed by nine o'clock in the evening and wake up at four o'clock in the morning, that's a strong seven hours of rest. Your body is rejuvenated, and you're up early to get things done before school starts, before the kids get up, before your spouse gets up, and before the sun comes up. Before the average person gets up, you've already hit the gym, run a few miles, written a chapter in that book you're working on, read a few chapters or pages of your favorite book, prayed, meditated, read or watched the news, checked emails, or worked on that new idea or business plan. By six thirty, you've done more than most average people have done before noon.

Option 2

Work late and get up early and do the same thing as the first option. You'll probably average about five hours of rest a night. Hopefully, you can find some time to take a few power naps throughout the day. Hopefully, you won't have to sacrifice your body for too long (two years, five years, maybe ten years) before you start giving your body the proper rest it needs.

Beasts

To be perfectly honest, some people will only get two or three hours of sleep. Some nights, they even do all-nighters. I call these people *beasts*. They are constantly in beast mode, meaning they will do whatever it takes to get the job done. They have passion, purpose, and an obsession for what they do. These people (a few just came to my mind) are usually great:

- Managers
- Administrators
- Presidents and owners of successful businesses
- Five-star athletes, all-pro athletes, Hall of Fame athletes
- A-list actors or hungry actors who want to make it
- Grammy Award winning artists
- Phenomenal teachers
- Excellent authors
- Incredible stay-at home-mothers and fathers
- Breathtaking motivational speakers
- Insightful doctors
- Groundbreaking researchers
- Amazing real estate agents

- Incredible chefs
- Awesome hair stylists
- Last but not least, these are the people who start off with absolutely nothing but a dream and a vision. These people are willing to work and die for their vision every single day!

Option 2 is probably the place where most successful people live for a long time before they can get back to earning seven to nine hours of rest. To be honest, those seven to nine hours for these people probably only come when they go on that much-needed and deserved vacation.

Get Up!

Our everyday habits will determine our futures. Take a moment to write down your everyday routine. Your routine will tell you if you are growing in the direction that you envision for your life. It will tell you if you're happy with your daily decisions. It will tell you if you're on the right track for greatness or if you're simply wasting time, confusing movement with progress. Your daily routine will talk to you, and only you, in a very personal and intimate way. Listen to it carefully. The one great thing about your daily routine is that it can always be tweaked and altered. What tweaks do you need to make? One tweak could possibly change your life forever. Success and failure comes down to inches.

Zombies

The other sleep that I mentioned are those people who are walking around sleepwalking. I compare them to the walking dead. They are zombies walking around following each other, trying their best to feed off of those who are conscious and have something they want. They have no direction and no purpose. They don't think for themselves. They let others control their destiny. They can see, but they have no vision. They can hear, but they never listen. It's impossible for them to lead because they always allow themselves to get pulled in a variety of different directions. They are followers twenty-four hours a day. They are content with having nothing they want or just a little bit of nothing. They are afraid of risk and failure. They are constantly angry, sad, worried, or stressed out, spending the majority of their lives in other people's business and never taking the time to create quality business of their own. The scariest thing about these zombies is that it's hard to tell who's who by just looking at them. Unlike the zombies we see on television, theses zombies know how to blend into our surroundings effortlessly. These, my friend, are the walking dead! They are real! Look around. They are living among us. If you're hanging around with zombies, you will eventually be bitten and become one yourself.

Whomever we hang around with the most will definitely influence us the most. It's way much better to keep company with those who inspire you, those who have something valuable to give, those whom you can learn from, those who have direction, those who have a loving (not a selfish) spirit, those who celebrate you and your accomplishments, those who know how to laugh at life, those who are not judgmental, those who encourage your ideas and dreams no matter how crazy they may seem, those who are on the grind, and those who are enjoying their journeys and happy to be on them. Instead of zombies, be bitten by a beast" and turn your life into whatever you want it to be.

The Weekends Are My Only Days to Sleep In

Really? These are definitely the best two days of the week to get a lot done. For example, if I know I'm going to be spending time with the family on Saturday, I get up at three o'clock in the morning and work until nine o'clock. That's six good hours to get work done before the day has truly begun for the day walkers. If I'm practicing for a golf tournament, I practice from six thirty in the morning to noon. I now have the rest of the day to do whatever it is I want to do with the family.

I mentioned writing a schedule for yourself a few chapters ago. Playing college and professional sports taught me how to write out a schedule. Our coaches always had us on a schedule. The itinerary was essential for us being on time for breakfast, dinner, treatment, pregame warm-up, an of course, bus and flight departures.

Writing out a schedule will help you organize your day and get you up so you can maximize every hour of the day. If you write your schedule out the night before, you'll always feel more prepared for the next day, no matter what. Don't waste your weekends in the bed. There's so much life to live. There so much to do. All I'm saying is, get your priorities taken care of early before you relax or spend time with the family on the weekends.

Sleep is the new broke!

~ Dr. Eric Thomas

~Notes~

15

_____
_____
_____
_____
_____
_____
_____
_____
_____
_____
_____
_____
_____
_____
_____
_____
_____
_____
_____
_____
_____
_____

If I Were Only Younger

16

If you do a little research, I bet you'll find a few people out there who did not care about how old they were when they started their journeys to achieve greatness at their crafts. Someone has done it before you. If they can do it, you can do it too. The question is, will you stay the course when things get tough and start to seem impossible to accomplish?

The reality is there will be a lot of pain and suffering involved in accomplishing our goals. There will be days when you feel like giving up. On those days, you have to believe there is a breakthrough coming right around the corner. There will be a lot of hours, days, weeks, months, and years when you'll have to sacrifice your time, sleep, and money. You will ask yourself, "What in the hell am I doing? I'm too old for this!" Your answer should be, "I'm doing what I was called to do. I'm doing what I'm supposed to be doing. I'm doing this for me. This is my vision, and I am going to make it my reality. I can't afford to stop. I can't afford to go backward. I started this journey, and I'm going to stay on this path no matter how narrow, dark, and rocky it gets."

Here's some good news. You will get a few less bruises during your journey if you have people in your corner who support you. Here are ten people who inspired and amazed me as I did a little research.

Samuel L. Jackson ~ Actor

Jackson graduated from Morehouse College in 1972. His first breakthrough on film came in 1991 in Spike Lee's *Jungle Fever* as a crack cocaine addict. He was forty-three years old at the time. Ironically, Jackson got this role days after completing rehab for cocaine use in his own personal life. In 1994, he broke out as a legitimate star when he played Jules in Quentin Tarantino's *Pulp Fiction* at the age of forty-six. In his long career, he has appeared in more than one hundred movies. His films have grossed more than $7 billion dollars worldwide. At the age of sixty-nine, he's still going stronger than ever and looking younger than ever. His net worth is in the neighborhood of $170 million. Side note: The odds of becoming a successful actor are 0.8 percent. He kicked the odds and age in the face and has never stopped kicking.

Fauja Singh ~ Marathon Runner

He is the world's oldest marathon runner at the age of 100. He has a British Empire Medal and a telegram from the Queen. At 92, he ran the marathon (26 miles) in five hours, 40 minutes. At 100, he ran the marathon in eight hours.

Ray Kroc ~ Business Man

He bought McDonald's at age fifty-two in 1954. He grew this company into the world's biggest fast-food franchise.

Taikichiro Mori ~ Real Estate Investor

He started investing in real estate at the age of fifty-one and founded Mori Building Company. In 1992, he was the richest man in the world with a net worth of $13 billion.

Stan Lee ~ Comic Book Writer

He created Spider-Man when he was forty-three and the Fantastic Four when he was forty-four.

Colonel Sanders ~ KFC

His chicken business idea was created when he was sixty-five years old. KFC is now one of the largest fast-food restaurant chains in the world. When he died in 1980, his net worth was $3.5 million. KFC is now in more than eighty countries, and the multiple franchises are making billions of dollars all around the world.

Sylvester Stallone ~ Actor, Director, and Writer, *Rocky* franchise, *Rambo* franchise, *The Expendables* franchise, *Creed*, and *Creed II*

Stallone was thirty years old when he wrote the script for the first *Rocky* film. He not only wrote the script but directed and starred in the movie as well. He saw the Muhammad Ali vs. Chuck Wepner fight one night and was inspired to write. After being homeless and sleeping in a bus terminal in New York City for three weeks, he had to make something happen or continue to suffer on the streets. To date, he has starred in more than fifty-four films in his career. He has a star on the Hollywood Walk of Fame, and his net worth as of 2017 was in the neighborhood of $500 million. He was thirty years old and continued to chase his dream. Now, he's living his dream because he never thought it was too late for his career to take flight.

Age Ain't Nothing but a Number.

~Aaliyah

~Notes~

16

I Don't Have Any Money

17

"I don't have any money!" This should be the best phrase in the world that motivates us to go out and get some. Some people may say money can't make you happy. I say, try living without it and see how that works for you. Some people say money is the root of all evil. It can be if we make bad decisions with it and because of it. Did you know that money is also the end result of people eating every day, wearing clothes, traveling, and having a roof over their heads? Being able to do and have these simple things makes me very happy.

If you don't have the money you need to do what it is you want, you need to ask yourself what is the best way (legally) to get it? Pick up a pen or pencil and start writing down all of the ideas and potential resources that come to your mind. Do you have any friends or family members who believe in what it is you're trying to accomplish and are willing and able to foot the bill? That may be an option for some, but for a large majority of people, taking out that student loan is the only option they have. You may have to bite the bullet and take out that business loan. You may have to work somewhere you hate until you save enough money and decide to jump to the next phase of your personal and financial evolution. No matter how difficult your circumstances may seem, never stop fighting and looking for ways to improve.

You never know where your next idea or learning experience will come from that will lead you to the financial resources you need. It could be a book, a YouTube video, or Google. Just keep grinding and searching for a way. I believe the universe says if you work hard, give maximum effort, listen, and try to help others along the way, the fruits of your labor will eventually start falling in your lap. The Bible says, "Ask and you shall receive. Seek and you shall find. Knock and the doors shall be open. Give and it shall be given unto you!" (Matthew 7:7 NIV Version). The simple principle of giving is amazing. Try it. Start giving your time to others. Start giving money to others. Start giving your ear to others. Start helping others, and watch how God starts opening doors that you never thought would be open. If you believe it, you can achieve it. Keep giving generously and working hard, and the money and opportunities will come.

People will start to notice your commitment, your hustle, and your dedication. People love helping people who inspire them in some way. Those who are in a position to help will come out of the shadows to help you toward your vision and goals. If they see potential, maximum effort, and a never-quit and positive attitude, they will definitely come for you. It only takes one helping hand to financially kick-start you on your journey of success—just one. You may get two hundred "No's" before you get that one "Yes." It's human nature for people to want to help or just be around winners. I believe when people see a winner in you, they bend over backward to help you. And yes, there will be others who will bend over backward to hate on you, but you can't let the haters derail you off of your winning path.

Help others, and help will come to you when you need it the most.

~Notes~

17

If I Only Had Someone to Help Me

18

No one is going to truly help you if you're not willing to help yourself. I tell my student athletes all of the time, "I can't want it more than you!" We have to be our own biggest cheerleaders. We have to be our own biggest critics. We have to be the biggest workaholics toward our own dreams and goals. Stop feeling sorry for yourself. Get up off of your butt, and stop crying about every damn thing. That gets nothing accomplished. No one cares about all of your complaints. Being depressed about your situation and doing nothing to change it will never get you what you want. I know it's hard, but if it wasn't hard, you'd already have what you want. Hard is part of the journey. The help will come when you're mentally and spiritually ready for it. Help is always looking for those trying to help themselves. Help is never looking to carry the entire load, but it is looking for you. The question is, are you ready for the help that is coming for you, or will it pass you by to help someone else who is ready for it?

The Bible says, "Faith without deeds is dead!" (James 2:14 NIV Version).

Faith (noun): Believing those things that are not as though they were. Believing something will happen before it does. Belief that is not based on proof.

Deed (noun): Something that is done, performed, or accomplished.

Start preparing yourself now. What books do you need to start reading? What motivational tapes or videos do you need to listen to? Who do you need to talk to that will answer questions that need to be asked by you? Help is coming. So in the meantime and in between time, get yourself ready, so help will get off the freeway and stop at your address.

It's better to be prepared with no opportunity, than to have an opportunity and not be prepared.

~ Les Brown

~Notes~

18

_____
_____
_____
_____
_____
_____
_____
_____
_____
_____
_____
_____
_____
_____
_____
_____
_____
_____
_____
_____
_____
_____

If I Lived in a Different Neighborhood, Things Would Be Different

19

You're absolutely correct. If you lived in a different neighborhood, things would be different. What are you doing now to get yourself closer to the neighborhood you really want to live in? What are you doing to make the neighborhood you do live in better, safer, and more festive? What changes can you make? What's going on? What do you actually see?

What I Saw

In the city of Compton where I was born and raised (1971–1989), I saw a lot of interesting things in my neighborhood. I saw crackheads running out of the projects, punching on poles, and running down the middle of the street trying to stop traffic. I saw crack cocaine in my hands with an opportunity to make a quick drop down the street. I saw nasty-looking prostitutes walking up and down Long Beach Boulevard. I saw gangbangers in all blue, dancing at parties in wheelchairs. I saw Piru gangbangers that could not utter a word that started with the letter *C*. I saw a guy pull up at a traffic light and shoot the back window out of the car in front of him, while my buddies and I were sitting at a bus stop. I saw corrupt leadership at the mayor's office in the city of Compton. I saw police demand that I get on my knees for no good reason. I saw myself being chased by bloods, while I was riding my bike in the wrong neighborhood. I saw myself get hit with a nightstick by a police officer at Compton College.

I also saw two-parent homes on almost every house on Chester block. I saw and experienced some good ass whupen's. I saw water balloon fights. I saw neighborhood block parties. I saw pop-locking dance battles. I saw backyard basketball games. I saw big wheels and dirt bikes on Christmas. I saw football games in the middle of the street. I saw fun hide-and-go-seek and hide-and-go-get-it games. I saw my buddy Beanie destroy everybody on the street in capping sessions. He had us laughing for hours.

- ❖ Yo mama got three legs. Caught her walking around in circles the other day.
- ❖ Yo mama so skinny, she be walking down the street falling through cracks.
- ❖ Yo mama glasses are so thick, when she looks at a map, she can see people waving.
- ❖ Yo mama so short, she got to cuff her panties.
- ❖ Yo mama so short, I can see her feet on her driver's license picture.
- ❖ Yo mama ain't got no feet. Always talking about let's go kick it.
- ❖ Yo mama play linebacker for the Chicago Lakers.
- ❖ Yo mama got three teeth. Two are in her back pocket.

I don't know if you laughed at any of these, but they were funny back in the day.

Anyway, I saw trips to the beach. I saw and experienced the best talent shows and sporting events at Roosevelt Junior High. I saw the best band ever play at Compton High School football games when I was twelve years old. I saw some of Compton High School's greatest football team's play between 1982 and 1984. I saw myself excel in every sport that I played. I saw myself with my own yard business at the age of fourteen. I saw myself catch four buses every morning to get to Carson High School (CA.) from the city of Compton. I saw myself buy my first car when I was seventeen. I saw NWA take the world by storm. I saw myself working at McDonald's all through high school. I saw money in my pocket. I saw myself earn a football scholarship.

I saw some of the best and worst that Compton had to offer. Compton built me. Compton is the foundation of my mental and spiritual growth. The good and the bad played equal parts in shaping my existence.

Wherever you live, you have to search for the good in your community. There is some good to be found everywhere we go. It might be hiding underneath rocks and behind buildings at times, but it's out there. Hopefully you can find good in your own home. If there's no good things happening there, try your best to find it somewhere else. It may be at a friend's house, at school, on the sports field, at the barber shop or hair salon, in a school club, or in the band. It may even be at work. But once you find it, hold on to it. That good will definitely help you find your way to a better experience in your neighborhood. That good will also help you find your way out of your neighborhood, if you have decided in your mind that you would prefer to live somewhere else in the future.

Try to embrace everything there is about your neighborhood. Learn from it. Learn from those around you. Embrace the daily sights and sounds that create that motion picture in your mind. Oftentimes, a lot of us have to *learn what not to do* in many cases. But learning is learning no matter what form it comes in. You must open your eyes to all of the many possibilities to change your experience from below average to average, from average to above average, from bad to good, and from good to great. Things have to be different in your mind before they can be different anywhere else.

Things have to be different in your mind first before
they can be different anywhere else.

~Notes~

19

I Can't Question Authority

20

If those who came before me had never questioned authority, I'd still be riding in the back of the bus. I wouldn't be able to vote. I wouldn't have been able to go to school with people who look different than I do. I wouldn't have been able to become CEO of my own company. I wouldn't be able to be a principal at a public school. There would be no African American head coaches in the NFL. Women tennis players wouldn't get paid the same prize money as their male counterparts.

The number of un-armed black boys and black men who are dying in the streets by the hands of ignorant and scared police officers would be even more astronomical. President Barack Obama would never have been the first African American president in the history of America. Lee Elders would have never played in the Masters. Tiger Woods would not have eighty-two PGA victories and fifteen majors. Jackie Robinson would never have played in the major leagues.

Change can only be made by those who are bold and fearless. They pursue change and equality as if their lives depended on it. *And they do.* They are scared in the face of the unknown but they battle the odds anyway.

If you never question or challenge those in authority, what is will always stay the same. No growth can happen, and the playing field will stay one-sided. Those in authority, believe it or not, are not always right. They are human beings just like you. As an administrator myself, I would love to be right all of the time, but I'm not. I'm glad I have people around me who are willing to speak their minds (respectfully) and tell me the truth by simply saying, "That's not right," or, "I disagree," and backing their statements up with quality arguments and facts. They keep me humble and more aware of what's going on around my campus.

Let's make this a little more personal. Do you have a teacher who's treating you like you're an idiot every day? Do you have a supervisor who disrespects you on a daily basis and talks down to you? Do you have a parent who treats you like you're still a little kid? Do you have a spouse or significant other who acts as if he or she has authority over you? Does that person make all major decisions for the family without consulting you? Do doctors, lawyers, managers, nurses, teachers, or police officers treat you as if your life means little or nothing? If so, take your power back, and speak your truth.

Compton's Finest ~ Playing Basketball on Our Knees

I was home from college one summer. A few of my buddies and I were in the backyard playing basketball. As we were in the heat of a game, two more of friends pulled up and walked back to where the games were being played. Two minutes later, two officers from the Compton Police Department pulled up. As they walked up, everyone stopped playing and just stared at them.

With a very authoritative voice, one of the officers said, "Everyone to the front."

We all walked to the front, confused about what was going on. We were all standing there, some of us with our shirts off, still sweating from the game.

So, of course, one of the officers says, "Everyone on your knees and put your hands on top of your heads!"

All of my buddies did exactly what was ordered except for (you guessed it) me.

I remember saying, "Officer, why are we getting on our knees. Have we broken any laws?"

He said, "Get on your knees!"

I replied, "I'm not getting on my knees because I have not broken any laws. So, if you want me on my knees, you're going to have to shoot me! What is your badge number, sir? I will be talking to your watch commander as soon as we're done here."

I remember my uncle coming out of the house and yelling, "Boy, get on your knees before they shoot your ass!"

I yelled back, "Get on my knees for what?! We've broken no laws! And I will be talking to their watch commander. This is ridiculous!"

The officer's claimed there was suspicious activity reported in the area.

My buddies were like, "Man why are you tripping? Just get down, Gat!"

I couldn't do it. By this time, it seemed like everyone on the street was standing outside on their porches or standing in front of their houses watching and listening to all of this unfold. After the officers and I had a few exchanges of words, they told everyone to get up.

The next day I went straight to the police station to talk with the watch commander, and he apologized for the officer's conduct. In the same breath, he said that there were pockets in the neighborhood where drugs were being sold. All I knew was that those drug sales had nothing to do with me or my buddies. We were just in the backyard enjoying a competitive game of basketball when these officers interrupted our game with their abusive style of community service.

After that entire situation was over, I knew I had to always stand for what I believed in. I knew I could never allow someone to treat me like a second-class citizen. I don't care if you are the president of the United States, you will treat me with respect.

I felt empowered and strong because of the stance I took that day. I made it a point to always stand up for myself and others in the future. Hopefully, my buddies and everyone who was watching will never forget that day. I was able to stand up for our rights and live to talk about it. Thank God the situation did not take a terrible turn for the worse like it did for Mike Brown, Alton Sterling, Walter Scott, Eric Garner, Philando Castile, Rekia Boyd, Michael Brown, Laquan McDonald, Akai Gurley, Tamir Rice, Freddie Gray, Eric Harris, William Chapman III, Sam DuBose, Jeremy McDole, Ricky Ball, and Jamar Clark.

As I'm writing this, I feel very proud of all of the people in our communities, who stand against the injustices in our country where police brutality and sexual harassment is overwhelming our communities and the government.

At some point, we must say enough is enough. Hopefully your breaking point comes sooner than later. If you're going through something right now and your voice stays silent, you are allowing these people or groups to consistently rob you of your true self. They are robbing you of better opportunities. They are robbing you of your true voice, of great ideas, of advancement, of productive relationships, and of true happiness. They are not only robbing you but robbing others around you who are not as strong as you are and are experiencing some of the same hurts, pains, and injustices.

You have to punch these people in the mouth (figuratively speaking) with boldness, awareness, and confidence in yourself. You have to use your voice and let these people know you are worthy of respect. Eventually, you will be treated with dignity. The day you stand up for yourself and let your voice be heard, is the first day you will truly be respected and things will start to change. Things may even change for the worse at first, but you will have established who you are. You will have established that you and others like you are worthy of respect. You will stand strong for others who are not yet strong enough to stand for themselves.

If you don't do this, you will always live as an unhappy person who will forever play the victim role until you get sick and tired of being sick and tired. The choice is yours.

When will you finally get sick and tired of being sick and tired?

~Notes~

20

I've Never Done That Before

21

You'll never know how great you are or how great you can be until you jump. As Steve Harvey would say, "We have to jump off the cliff of the unknown throughout life, if we want to truly discover and develop the gifts and passions that God has placed inside of us. You have to jump, if you want to discover the person inside of you that is starving for true happiness and joy. You're going to hit some rocks and mountains on the way down and get scraped up. It's going to hurt like hell too. But eventually, if you keep free falling to greatness, your parachute will open and you will start to glide and soar with the eagles."

I think Steve Harvey may know a few things about struggle, homelessness, being broke, following his dream, and persevering through very dark days and coming out on top.

Play it safe, or take a risk? Those who play it safe will always have what they have—nothing more, nothing less. Those who take risk will enjoy the pain and joy of the journey. They are just inches away from greatness, or they are living in their dreams and enjoying every minute of the good, the bad, and the ugly of their greatness. They consistently live day to day in a consistent state of mind, knowing that they are exhausting every mental and physical effort to stay in their calling and their purpose.

These risk-takers eventually learn how to live debt-free and are able to spend and save their money wisely. They fight and claw their way from living paycheck to paycheck like so many of us do. Look, none of this comes easy, so you must continue to fight through the pain and suffering of multiple life situations until they reach victory.

> *When you jump off of the cliff, you're going to fall and get scraped up; but eventually your wings will open and you will start to fly.*
> ~ Steve Harvey

~Notes~

21

My Kids Won't Let Me

Personally, this is a tough one for me to touch. I didn't have any biological kids of my own, so putting my personal goals and aspirations on hold because I had to raise kids is not my reality.

But, I do believe that everyone is entitled to follow their dreams and goals, no matter what the circumstances. I just want to say, please don't let any more time go by before you start working on what's important to you. One article at time. One page at a time. One class at a time. Take as many baby steps as possible, and eventually, you will start walking with confidence and running with power. I've come to believe that kids should be a big part of our lives, not all of our lives.

My life's work is working with other people's kids, so I definitely understand the complexities that families face in this new world we live in where instant gratification is king. The deception of instant gratification is creating a generation of kids who feel entitled to everything without putting in the work.

If you really start to organize your day and write out a schedule minute by minute, I bet you'll find a little bit of time to work on your own dreams and passions in between nursing, cleaning up, picking the kids up from school, dropping them off at practice, going to games, cooking dinner, helping with homework, going to plays, and paying money for hundreds of other things. There are twenty-four hours in a day, and I guarantee you that some of that time is meant just for you. You just have to find those minutes and hold on to them. Those minutes will eventually turn into hours if you stick with your passions and your dreams long enough.

I have a full-time job as a principal, but I still set goals for myself every day. My kids (my students) take up a large part of my day. I'm at work from 6:45 a.m. until 4:00 p.m. Sometimes I have to stay until 7:00, 8:00, or 9:00 p.m., depending on if I have to make an unexpected home visit, find a missing student, work on schedules, work on budgets, or simply have to stay at school for a sporting event, dance, or band concert. *Sind Note: I used to stay at school for sporting events, dances and band concerts. Now, I'm the principal at a community day school for behavioral, social, and emotionally challenged students.*

Just like you, I have to figure out where I'm going to get the time to do other things that I'm passionate about. I knew if I ever wanted to finish this book, I would not only have to write on the weekends, but I would have to get up at 2:30, 3:30, and 4:30 a.m., to write before I went to the gym and then to work.

I also know if I want to play serious tournament golf and drop my handicap from a seven to a zero, I have to create the time to train with my swing coach. I now have to put the practice hours in after work, on weekends, on holidays and during the summer months.

We have to refuse to let our kids take our dreams and goals away from us. Our dreams are ours and ours alone. God gave them to us and we should grab hold of them and never let them go. We must fight for our own personal time every day. It's ours!

I am entitled to follow my dreams and develop my gifts.

~Notes~

22

Money Won't Make
Me Happy

23

I don't know about you, but here are a few things regarding money that make me happy. Here's a short list:

- When I'm eating food I bought with my own money
- When I walk out of the house with a nice suit on or some nice jeans and a nice shirt
- When I'm rocking a brand new pair of *Air Jordan's*
- When I can take my wife out for date night
- When I drive my SUV and don't have to catch the bus to work
- When I come home from a long day at work and walk into *my house*, sit down on *my couch*, and turn on Sports Center
- When I play in golf tournaments that cost money
- When I can pay the mortgage, gas, electric, trash, phone, and cable bill on time every month
- When I'm able to provide for my family (My manhood is deeply connected to me being able to have money and provide for my family.)
- When I can help those in need with my money

Obviously, to do or have all of these things, it takes money. Most people who say, "Money won't make me happy," usually don't have any. If we use money wisely, we can be very happy and create a future for ourselves and our families. The more money we obtain, the more money we have to help ourselves and others we care about.

Does money bring out the worst or best in people? I believe it depends on the person. I also believe money brings out the truth about what you value. For example, if you value things that will appreciate in the future like, people, homes, savings accounts, stocks, business, and books, your money will go a long way and you're money will provide happy times. If you put too much value into things like clothes, phones, jewelry, cars, and entertainment, your money will not last long at all. But this is the truth about people: We all have different values. The values that we have will either make us or break us whether we have tons of money or not. Will we choose to live below or above our means? Will we choose to spend, spend, spend or save as we go?

To be honest with you, I struggle in certain areas of my finances. I have to get better just like some of you. I will continue to read self-help financial books, communicate with those who are highly financially literate, and set small goals that will enhance my experiences with money and life.

This I do know: You will never have to worry about having money, if you don't grind and work hard at developing a skill that a company or customers will pay you for. Money is the number-one reason why most people go to school, college, trainings, sports camps, and seminars.

In my opinion, money can make us happy for a long time, or it can make us happy for a brief moment. It all depends on what we value. It depends on the weaknesses and strengths of our financial literacy. I have a quote hanging up in my garage that reads: "Money without financial intelligence, is money soon gone!" It slaps me in my face every time I read it!

Here's a few great resources on money management.
- *The Total Money Makeover* by Dave Ramsey
- *Unshakeable: Your Financial Freedom Playbook* by Tony Robbins
- *Rich Dad Poor Dad* by Robert T. Kiyosaki

Money without financial intelligence, is money soon gone!
~ Robert T. Kiyosaki

~Notes~

23

_____
_____
_____
_____
_____
_____
_____
_____
_____
_____
_____
_____
_____
_____
_____
_____
_____
_____
_____
_____
_____
_____
_____
_____
_____

My Significant Other Won't Support Me (For Grown Folks)

24

If you don't have a supportive spouse or significant other, your goals and dreams will be very, very hard to achieve. Let me just say, I'm very blessed to have a wife who supports what I do. Again, if you do not have the support you need at home, it will be difficult, but you can still accomplish your goals if you have the right mind-set and a never-quit, beast mode work ethic. I believe we must first sit down with our significant others and lay out our plans, our goals, and our visions and have a solid conversation about how important this is and how best to attack it. Does it make financial sense right now? If not, what is it that you need to do in order to pay for those classes, that seminar, that website, those book publishing fees, those tournament fees, or that start-up money for that business.

Hopefully, after a good long conversation and showing your spouse or significant other your plan of attack, he or she will have a better understanding of what it is you are trying to accomplish and why. Most people can better visualize and understand a concept when he or she can see the plan, the vision, the cost, and the small- and long-term goals written down on paper.

If you go to your spouse or significant other with this rough draft and he or she sees how passionate you are, you have a better chance of that person seeing bits and pieces of your vision. Now, if you have done all you can do to show and explain what you want to accomplish and he or she is still negative, pessimistic, and unsupportive, then you may need to see if the other person is willing to go to some type of counseling. If you guys can get a third perspective on the situation, hopefully that will help shed more light and perspective on your vision.

Your spouse or significant other is an important part of your life, so it helps when that person supports your dreams. But let me say this: never expect full support if you're not fully committed to your own dream. Your significant other will see that right away and not give you the full support that you are seeking. No one can want what you want for yourself more that you do. You can't expect help and support if you're not willing to sacrifice your own money and time.

If the support is not there, you will simply have to show your partner how serious you are. Continue to grind and do the things you need to do. Hopefully, he or she will get on board once you make it clear how committed you are.

In most cases, this may cause high levels of stress and strain on the relationship. This is something you will have to fight through. You have to be a fighter. You have to fight for your dreams and fight for your relationship if the relationship is worth fighting for.

Never kill your dreams for someone else. You will regret it for the rest of your life. Do everything that you can possibly do to make your dreams come true. If you do that, and for some reason it does not pan out at the end of your journey, hopefully you'll be able to say, "I did everything I could do and the experience alone made me a better person. It showed me how strong and how smart I can really be. I have no regrets and because of this experience, I'm richer now than I've ever been."

Les Brown, who is a great motivational speaker, once said, "Imagine if you will, that you were on your deathbed in the hospital and standing around you were all of these angry faces. The faces represent all of the ideas, dreams, and visions you had in your life time. They start talking to you saying, 'We are so angry, because we now have to die with you. You never gave us birth, and now the world will never know who we are or what we could have accomplished. They will never know the many lives we could've affected. We are pissed at you! We hate you for never caring about us enough, to give us life!'"

After I heard this with my own ears, there was no way I could just sit back and not finish my book campaign. If just one person changes his or her mind-set after reading at least one sentence that I've written, my legacy will be cemented here on earth forever.

I don't know about you, but that is one of the scariest stories I've ever heard. I definitely don't want that to happen to me. We must continue to fertilize and water our ideas so the world can benefit—so we can benefit. Our minds, our spirits, our souls, our bodies, and, eventually, our bank accounts will benefit if we stay the course.

> *The wealthiest place in the world, is the graveyard.*
> *Will your great ideas die with you?*
> ~ Les Brown

~Notes~

24

No One in My Family Has Ever Done It Before

So what?! You be the first to ever do it then. Lead by your actions, not by your mouth. As soon as you take the first step, others will follow. Your siblings are looking up to you. Your kids are looking up to you. Your friends are looking up to you. Be the first to make a difference in your family. Be the first to break the cycle of fear and self-doubt. Someone is counting on you to take the first step, so he or she can muster up the courage to be as courageous as you.

I'm proud to share with you that I was the first and only person in my family of five brothers and one sister to ever go to college. I was the first and only person in my family to earn an athletic scholarship. I was the first to live in Europe. I was the first to buy five houses in the same year. I was the first and only to get my master's degree, and I am the first and only person in my family to ever write a book.

Once you step out on faith and do what you know you need to do, other firsts will get easier and easier, and before you know it, you will have a long list of accomplishments that you never thought you could accomplish. You will inspire those who are most important to you in your family, and you will prove your doubters and your haters wrong.

If not you, then who? If not now, then when? Don't let your dreams and ideas die with you. Leave them here for others to enjoy. Inspire those around you to be even greater. No more excuse! Get it done! You have to be the first because this thing you want to conquer is your destiny waiting for you. Your destiny and your passions are waiting for you and only you. Do you feel the empty void inside of you? I know you feel it. If you didn't feel it, you would not be reading this chapter right now. And I know somebody flipped straight through the book to read this chapter first. This chapter is slapping you in the face right now. It's challenging you to get up off of your butt and do what it is you know you need to do.

Is it going to be hard? Hell yes! Is it going to be challenging? Yes! Are you going to have people telling you you're crazy? Yes sir! Are you going to cry behind closed doors many nights? Yes ma'am! Are you going to want to quit sometimes? Will you be scared? Without a doubt! Courage is when you're scared to do something but you do it anyway. Are you going to succeed? Yes! Your success is already in your mind, heart, and spirit. Pull it out and grind it like coffee beans. Be the first to be great in your family. Be the first to change and take charge of your life. Be the first to take risks and live freely with the consequences of your decisions. Be the first to …

- Go to college
- Go back to school
- Buy that house
- Start that business
- Try out for the team
- Get on that stage
- Go to that audition
- Write that book
- Start that music label
- Travel out of the country
- Make that investment
- Start that band
- Apply for that job
- Enter that tournament

Do you! But … what if … Stop it. Don't be your own biggest roadblock. You are the only person who can stop you from changing your circumstances. No one is going to believe in you more than you. *Have no regrets.*

> *A man is not old until regrets take the place of dreams.*
> ~ John Barrymore

~Notes~

25

I Don't Feel Like It

26

Really? You don't feel like it? You will never get anything done if you always operate on how you feel. Your emotions will steer you wrong every time. Too many people get caught up in their feelings and emotions too often and forget the purpose of the daily journey. I get up in the morning between three and four o'clock in the morning. Sometimes I get up at two thirty, depending on what project I'm working on. Remember, I actually wrote 90 percent of this book between the hours of two thirty and six o'clock in the morning.

Do I feel like getting up that early every morning? No. Some mornings I'm dead tired and my doubts start to creep in, but I know I have to get up because the success of my journey depends on it. My passion for the project gets me up more than anything. My future depends on it. My family depends on it. My health depends on it. My dreams and ideas depend on it. I've made a promise to myself that my dreams and ideas will not die with me. They will live long after I'm gone. When we start letting our emotions take control of our actions, we start taking the life out of our bodies, one breath at a time.

One hundred percent of the time, our dreams, goals, and passions should get us out of bed before the alarm clock goes off. We should be excited about the possibility to approach another day with our vision. No matter how small or big that vision is, it's ours to cultivate and allow to grow.

I get it, I get it. Some days you are going to feel like quitting, killing your momentum and killing your dreams because nothing seems to be going right. Doors are being shut in your face. People who are closest to you are doubting you. Those closest to you are stabbing you in the back. You're starting to doubt yourself. You're starting to think about how crazy you are for trying to attempt this crazy journey. You're even starting to think about how much time and money you've spent so far. Please, let those thoughts pass through your mind like a football flying down the field and landing incomplete to its intended receiver.

These are the days you have to say to yourself, "I'm getting close. Greatness is right around the corner. My breakthrough is coming! This pain is only temporary! What can I learn from this?" You have to think about all of the work you've put in so far. There is no turning back at this point.

As an aspiring professional golfer, I get beat up by the process on a daily basis. I get frustrated because some days I tell myself that I don't see any growth. What the hell am I doing out here? I shoot a seventy-five one day and an eighty-one the next. I ask myself, "When will I consistently shoot below par?" The truth is, I grow every time I pick up a club. I learn what works and what doesn't work on every single shot. The more I work, the more pain I experience, but I do know the pain is only temporary, and I will use those experiences to help me get better in the future. I continue to remind myself that I must continue to study the game, work with my swing coach, and bounce back strong after a bad shot or bad decision.

Do you realize that I just shared one of my dreams with you? Only a few people know about this dream of mine. Now you know. I play in golf tournaments all over Southern and Northern California.

- Simi Hills Men's Championship
- LA City Men's Championship
- LA County Men's Championship
- Pasadena Men's Championship
- Long Beach City Men's Championship

- Oakland City Men's Championship
- Oxnard City Men's Championship

The highest I've ever placed to date is third place, but I am determined to one day consistently shoot under par and start winning tournaments. You may be thinking, *He's crazy.* If you're a golfer, you may be thinking, *He's only shooting seventy-five. Does he know how good those guys are?* See, crazy people don't think like everyone else. We see the vision and push forward no matter the odds. The only reason I shared this with you is so you can hopefully be inspired to dream big as well. I'm just like you. I have dreams and goals I have yet to accomplish. If for some reason I don't make it on that big stage, I will still be forever changed and a better golfer and person than I could've ever imagined.

Hopefully, you will *feel* like getting up every day to chase your dreams. No matter how crazy your dreams may be, keep pushing forward. If we shoot for the moon and miss, we'll still be among the stars. The challenges and scrapes and bruises alone will change us forever.

I'm sure Michael Jordan didn't feel like playing in game six of the NBA playoffs in 1998 against the Utah Jazz, when he had the flu. He came out anyway and scored thirty-six points, leading the bulls to victory and their fifth NBA championship. His teammates actually had to carry him off of the court when the game was over.

I'm sure Bill Gates didn't feel like starting a new company by the name of Microsoft after his first business by the name of Traf-O-Data failed.

I'm sure Albert Einstein didn't feel like studying when his teachers thought he was mentally handicapped, slow, and antisocial after they expelled him from school. He persevered through it all. Despite all of the doubts and low expectations people had of him, he pushed through because he didn't let his feelings and emotions take control of his life. He was able to continue his journey and convincingly prove the naysayers wrong by eventually winning the Noble Prize and changing the face and thought process of modern physics.

As a little girl, I'm sure Oprah Winfrey didn't feel like getting up most mornings. She had to deal with a sexually abusive childhood. She also had to deal with getting pregnant at the age of fourteen because of multiple sexual assaults. She even had to overcome losing her baby shortly after birth. I'm sure her self-esteem and confidence took a devastating hit during that time period. But she kept getting up and coming back for more of what the world had to dish out.

Look at Oprah now. She had the most successful talk show in history. Oprah's Master Class is still airing. She's now the CEO of OWN network and *OWN* magazine. She's an incredible actress, producer, and a best-selling author. She's opened her own schools for inspiring youth, and most importantly, she's able to help so many people around the world with her generous philanthropic heart.

I'm sure President Obama didn't feel like dealing with the media or Congress half the time. It was incredible to see how certain members of Congress would disrespect him and his authority by making disrespectful comments during congressional meetings and media press conferences. President Obama was a true professional and took it all in stride. He took the advice of his wife, Michelle Obama. "When they go low, you go high!" He got up every day to face whatever came his way, whether he felt like it or not. President Obama, the first African American president in the history of the United States, which was founded in 1776, was an incredible president and a better human being. It took 232 years before America was ready for an African American president. When his number was called, he was ready and willing. There had to many days he didn't feel like dealing with ignorance, hatred, and jealousy from colleagues who did not approve of his position, his title, his power, and his skin color.

I'm sure single mothers and fathers don't feel like going to work every day, but they get up anyway because they have mouths to feed. They don't feel like going to every football game, basketball game, or band performance, but they do it anyway because their children's confidence and support structure is more important than their feelings.

The most important question we all have to ask ourselves at some point is; *What is my why?* Why do I get up every morning? Why am I going back to school? Why am I working two jobs? Why am I saving this money? Why am I going to the gym or yoga class four or five days a week? Why am I going to therapy? Why am I starting this new business? Why am I running stadium bleachers or running sand dunes at four o'clock in the morning?

What is your *why*? Rather you feel like it or not, your why will always push you to get up and do whatever it is you need to do to continue your important journey.

Your why has to be very important to you if you're going to get up and do something that you don't feel like doing sometimes. No one can want it more than you. You must be obsessed with your passion, and your why should drive you to the finish line every day.

My "Why" is the only thing that will push me to greatness, not my Emotions.
~ Dr. Eric Thomas

~Notes~

26

My Skin Is Too Dark

27

Boys to Men ~ Light versus Dark

Your skin is too dark for what? Is your skin not the right complexion to be the president of the United States of America? Is your skin not the right complexion to be a model, to date whomever you want, to run a company, to own your own business, to make quality friends, to live in *that* community, or to do whatever it is you decide to work for? Don't let society, magazines, and television define who you are and what you can accomplish in this life. We have to look in the mirror and embrace who we are.

I've seen a variety of students sitting across from my desk over the years with low self-esteem because of the way they look. As parents, mentors, brothers, sisters, teachers, and coaches, we have to start recognizing what's going on with our children. Our boys are crying out for help just as much as our little girls.

I was light skinned back in 1977–78 before I started going to the beach a lot. Just joking! When I was in elementary school, kids used to talk about my skin complexion all of the time. You're so black, you have to smile at night, so people can see you. You're so black, when you bend over, you look like a crowbar. You're so black, you have to put on white gloves when you eat tootsie rolls so you won't bite your fingers off. I've heard them all.

I don't think the name-calling affected me as much as other kids because I could always think about my mother. Her skin was dark like mine and I always thought she was the most beautiful woman I'd ever seen. So when I looked in the mirror as a kid, I always saw my mom in me. I also had a lot of mama jokes in my repertoire to back my peers up off of me when needed. But they did make me question why I was so dark every now and then.

The worst insult I ever received was in my sophomore year of high school. One day I was walking to football practice with my shoulder pads and helmet in my hands. I was approaching two girls about fifty yards away from the boys' locker room. As I got closer to them, one of the girls said, "Excuse me. Do you play football?"

I said, "Yeah!" I was feeling myself a little bit.

And then one of them said, "Damn, you're so skinny and black!" They started laughing and walked off.

I walked away feeling about two feet tall. I could take it from the boys, but at that age, hearing it from girls was a dagger. I was used to the black jokes from the fellas, but the girls' black-and-skinny comments cut me to the core. I admit, I was very slim (6 feet and 165 pounds), but damn they could've kept those hurtful comments to themselves.

So, of course, I started drinking milk and lifting weights five days a week like a beast. It's funny how the opposite sex can motivate you to do certain things faster than you normally would. By the time I was a senior, I was 180 pounds and ripped up like Bruce Lee. If you don't know who Bruce Lee is, please do a quick internet search on him. He was my superhero growing up. We kind of look alike if you close one eye. Anyway, I used their words as motivation. Haters can definitely inspire you. I say, use whatever you need to get you over the hump. Thank you, ladies. In the words of Frenchie from *In Living Color*, "Don't love me like you do!"

As a teenage boy in the late eighties and early nineties, I have to admit, there were a few celebrities that made it extra cool to be dark skinned. Bobby Brown (the bad boy from New Edition), Michael Jordan, Full Force, Wesley Snipes, Kool Moe Dee, Big Daddy Kane, Play (from Kid 'n Play), and Tyrese (way before the crying spell on social media).

I remember a comedian saying, "Back in the day, before certain celebrities made it cool to be dark, dark-skinned brothas couldn't get a date until Black History Month!" Celebrities like El DeBarge and Al B. Sure! made it tough on dark skin brothas. We all know (which is really sad) that in every generation, celebrities pave the way for what is hot and what is not, from clothes, shoes, houses, cars, jewelry, and, unfortunately, skin color. So, of course, today we have celebrities like Morris Chestnut, Taye Diggs, Idris Elba, Darrin Henson, and Ne-Yo, representing for the dark-skinned brothas. Sadly, they have to remind the world that it's okay to be dark-skinned and that you can treat us like everyone else.

I do have to admit, light-skinned celebrities are still stronger than ever, with the likes of Boris Kojoe, Terrence Howard, Brian White, Laz Alonso, T.I., LL Cool J, Jon Legend, Columbus Short, and Michael Ealy. If you don't recognize some of these names, please do a quick internet search. Ladies, you won't be disappointed at all.

I make light of this somewhat, but historically, dark and light-skinned black folks have been psychologically pitted against one another for decades. During slavery, we had dark-skinned field negros who worked in the fields doing hard labor, and we had light-skinned house negros who worked in the master's house and received certain white privileges, one being learning how to read. Light-skinned black folks were considered less threatening, smarter, and better looking. Sadly, a lot of people in our society still believe that to be true today.

To my surprise, bleaching of the skin has now become popular among people of color, but only a few will admit it. As Americans, we still struggle with this psychological colorism each and every day. Unfortunately, black celebrities have a huge influence on American culture when it comes to how certain people react, respond, and treat us. Black celebrities also tend to have a huge influence on how we feel about ourselves and what we think we can or cannot accomplish in this game we call life.

Black Boys

On another note, black boys are suffering because a lot of them are not being celebrated for their small accomplishments. I strongly believe greatness is in the details. Low expectations are oftentimes the norm in many schools and communities for black boys. Confidence and work ethic in black boys is also lacking because of the large statistical numbers of absent fathers in the home. They need reassurance, structure, and mentoring from strong male role models. If we want their self-worth and belief in themselves to improve and soar, we must be willing to put in the work to better understand their individual stories, so we can create productive interventions and teaching opportunities that will propel them into a different mind-set that is rooted in love for self, education, service, and community.

Penn State

The American prison system is full of black and brown boys. The statistics are staggering. The likelihood of black boys and men that will go to prison is one in three. Black people make up 6.5 percent of the US population but make up 40.2 percent of the prison population. Our prison population has gone from 196,441 in 1970 to nearly 2.3 million today.

Take a moment to think about the decades of wrongful convictions, bad prison legislation, unbalanced justice, the mystical war on drugs, gang violence, police brutality, murder in the name of policing, fatherless homes, overpopulated prisons, boys and men locked up for crimes they didn't commit, imprisonment and murdering of strong black leaders, illegal distribution of guns in America's inner cities, as well as abandonment and bad decisions by undereducated and misinformed youth. This is a reality that we all must face and take accountability for each and every day.

The year is 1948! We must wake up! I'm sorry. The year is 1958! Sorry once again. It's been a long morning of writing. My mind is all over the place. I'm so sorry. We all know the actual year is 2020. Seriously, 2020!

I'll say this: if you are a young man, please start surrounding yourself with positive friends, family members, and mentors who will lift you up and celebrate you and all of your unique features, qualities, and accomplishments. Take every opportunity that comes your way to make a better way. Don't let your circumstances define your future. Don't let your misinformed friends define who you are, the decisions you make, and the person you choose to become. Every boy of color needs a survival kit to make it in today's society. If I were talking to a group of young men right now, I would share this survival kit with them.

Survival Kit ~ Sons

1. Men/boys must learn how to compete. You must give your best at everything you do. Nothing is free. You have to be three times better than those you are competing against.
2. Regarding credit: Live below your means. Debt will destroy your financial freedom.
3. Regarding hygiene: Take a shower or bath every day. Brush your teeth and floss. You'll need them when you get older. Put on deodorant and comb or brush your hair every day.
4. Regarding sex: No means *no*. Never force yourself on a girl or woman. If you can't afford to take care of yourself or your responsibilities, try your best not to engage in sexual activity at all. Always protect yourself.
5. Never hit a girl or woman. That's what cowards do.
6. If you mess it up, clean it up.
7. Regarding the police: Keep your hands where they can see them. No sudden movements.
8. Regarding work ethic: If you have no work ethic, you will always be broke.
9. Smile more, and frown less.
10. You will become a slave if you go to jail.
11. Listen more than you speak.
12. Once you push send, you never get that picture or text back.
13. Never disrespect your mother. That's what cowards do.
14. People will judge you because of your complexion, so you must have thick skin.
15. Speak boldly and with confidence.
16. Pray and meditate on positive affirmations daily.
17. If you love the streets, the streets will never love you back.
18. Choose your friends wisely. They are a reflection of you.
19. You must learn how to code switch when needed. (Speech & Movement)
20. Always give a firm handshake. It says a lot about your confidence. You will be judged by that handshake when you least expect it.
21. Do not depend on a woman to take care of you.

22. Most alcoholics took their first drink as a teenager.
23. Don't hang out in public with your black friends in huge packs.
24. The clothes you put on every day become your uniform. How do you want your uniform to represent you out in public?
25. When you become a man, it is your responsibility to take care of yourself, your responsibilities, and your family. You are the alpha male. Protect what's yours.
26. Watch the following two Netflix programs along with the listed movie. They're a must watch!

   ❖ *13th*. This film explores the history of racial inequality in the United States. It focuses on our nation's prison systems that are disproportionately filled with African Americans. Director: Ava DuVernay.
   ❖ *When They See Us*. This is a drama series based off of a true story. Five black teenagers wrongly accused and convicted of assault and rape of a woman jogger back in 1989 in New York City. Director: Ava DuVernay.
   ❖ *Brian Banks*. This is a movie based on a true story about a high school football star (from Long Beach Poly) who was falsely accused of rape. Starring: Aldis Hodge.

You have to stand strong and be proud of who you are and what you see in the mirror. Do whatever needs to be done to accomplish your goals. You will have to work two, three, or even ten times harder than some, but so be it. Do what you have to do and let nothing hold you back. We should feel proud of who we are and what we look like. It is a must that we go out into the world and create a significant life that is worthy of living, despite the many obstacles that we face.

Parents ~ Mentors ~ Teachers ~ Coaches

As leaders, I believe we must start opening up the lines of communication with one another. Community members, business owners, pastors, law-enforcement officers, city officials, teachers, and school administrators need to work together. We need to have town hall meetings and start looking at whatever data is out there, so we can better figure out what direction and what interventions are needed to help guide our youth and change destructive mind-sets of our teenagers and the biased minds-sets of adults who have power and influence.

Mentoring Programs for Boys

- 100 Black Men (www.100blackmen.org)
  This is the largest network of African American male mentors in the nation. They provide services in education, health and wellness, economic empowerment, and leadership development.
- The Boys to Leaders Foundation (www.boystoleadersfoundation.org)
- Concerned Black Men (www.cbmla.org)
  All of these organizations will empower, motivate, and inspire young men by providing leadership training; educational programs; and positive, personal, and professional development.

Girls to Women

In my opinion, I believe we live in a male chauvinistic society where there's usually a double standard for men and boys. Women and girls are judged at an extremely higher rate. Little girls and women are constantly reminded through friends, family, social media, videos, and magazines, that their appearance should look a certain way to be recognized by boys/men, and society. It's a shame how multitudes of people believe that girls/women have to look a certain way to be recognized as smart or intelligent.

Boys and men don't have to go through as much scrutiny as girls and women. Social media and magazines are not constantly telling boys and men that their hair has to be a certain length or they have to be a certain body size or shade. We pretty much get a free pass when it comes to our appearance in some social gatherings. We could even walk around looking dirty and dingy, and someone will say, "I like that rough and rugged look! He must work hard."

Ladies, please, stop listening and believing everything you see, hear, and read on social media, magazines, and television. You are beautiful human beings, especially your dark skin. Embrace it and own it. It's not going anywhere. If you walk with confidence and believe in who you are, incredible people will be attracted to you and what you have to offer. Whatever you give the universe, it will send back to you. Whatever you are trying to accomplish will happen for you if you just believe in you first. Surround yourself with positive girls and women who celebrate you for who you are.

The Doll Test

I thought it would be relevant for this chapter that I mention the doll test first conducted back in the 1940s. For those who are not familiar with the test, here's a brief history. According to some of the research done by the NAACP's Legal Defense and Education Fund Organization, the research reminds us of psychologists Kenneth and Mamie Clark who designed and conducted a series of experiments known as the doll tests to study the psychological effects of segregation of African American children. During the experiments, black children were given two dolls and were asked different questions.

- Show me the doll that you like best or that you'd like to play with.
- Give me the doll that looks like you.
- Give me the doll that looks like a Negro child.
- Give me the doll that looks bad.
- Show me the doll that is nice.

The subjects were children between the ages of three and seven. They were asked to identify both the race of the dolls and which color doll they preferred. A large majority of the kids preferred the white doll and assigned positive characteristics to it.

In 2005, Kiri Davis an African American filmmaker repeated the experiment in Harlem as part of her short film *A Girl Like Me*. She asked twenty-one children, and 71 percent told her that the white doll was nice and pretty and the black doll was bad. 2005! The objective of the test was to see how far our society has come in its attitude toward race, prejudice, belief patterns, and positive teaching strategies since the 1940s.

The results of both tests concluded that prejudice, discrimination, segregation, and negative stereotypes create feelings of inferiority among African American children and damage their self-esteem. According to the similarities of the tests, it does not seem that we've made huge strides (collectively) when it comes to attitudes and belief patterns concerning this issue.

I mention this test to show that there has been a very long history of psychological abuse and damaged self-esteem of boys and girls of color for many decades, especially little girls with dark skin who grow up to be women with dark skin. The same damaging messages from the past are just as damaging through social media, television, and magazines in today's new millennium. The message that dark skin is less attractive, less admirable, and less capable than lighter skin is still deeply rooted in our society.

We also must stop psychologically abusing our own children. It makes no sense if we are calling our little girls names, supporting what the media is saying. Example: "Get your black, ugly a——— in the house!" We all know there are a lot of homes where the adults are consistently verbally abusing the kids and expecting them not to act out or feel angry or depressed. How do we expect them to have high self-esteem? How do we expect them to believe in themselves?

It's very hard for our little girls to believe in themselves when they are being verbally abused on a daily basis by the very people who are taking care of them and claiming to love them. Some of us may also be showing them the same dysfunctional love that we were given as a child. Whatever that looks like! I believe it's very rare to see little girls who were verbally abused at home, grow into successful women who hold themselves in high esteem. Do get me wrong. It can be done, and it has been done but it is rare. All of us must continue to fight for the self-esteem of our little girls who may be ashamed of what they look like or who they are, because of the mixed messages that society and close circles of friends and family feed them on a daily basis.

The R. Kelly Syndrome

If you have not seen *Surviving R. Kelly*, please find some time in your schedule to watch it. It's a six-episode documentary on the Lifetime network. It first aired in January 2019. I personally believe it's a great opportunity for parents and daughters to sit down and watch together. The documentary is based on personal allegations of mental, physical, and sexual abuse of primarily black women. Most of whom were young under-aged, impressionable teens during the alleged abuse and trauma. These women give different accounts of how they were manipulated and sexually taken advantage of (for years) by a grown man and his employees. The underage girls ranged from fourteen to seventeen years old. You will also hear from counselors and psychologist on how the manipulation cycle is given birth years before the victims even meet their predators.

Warning: This documentary will shock and anger you. Please be ready to have some honest conversations with your daughters as you watch this series. If we as parents, family members, and educators don't take the time to educate, uplift, support, and remind our daughters of how capable, smart, and beautiful they are, they will continue to go out into the world and search for that affirmation from other sources. Those other sources come in the form of teenage boys, teenage girls, grown men or women, television, magazines, and social media. No matter how uncomfortable it may be, we have to open up the lines of communication, so we can save our daughters from being manipulated by predators and the negative ideologies of those that are ignorant, selfish, or trying to gain something and take something from our little girls. If I had a group of young ladies in my presence at this very moment, I would share with them my survival kit for young black and brown girls.

Survival Kit ~ Daughters

1. The world does not care about you, your excuses, or your problems.
2. Regarding credit: Live below your means. Your financial future depends on it. Debt will slowly suck the life out of you.
3. Regarding hygiene: Every day take a bath or shower and put on deodorant. Brush and floss your teeth two to three times a

day. You'll need your teeth when you get older. A great smile is priceless. Keep your nails and toes done. Feminine hygiene: Talk to your mother, grandmother, or auntie.

4. Regarding boys: You have all of the power. Wherever your standards are, boys with the same standards will find you. Your body is a Mercedes Benz. Don't give anyone the keys until you are grown and responsible enough to take care of yourself and your responsibilities.

5. Keep your bathroom clean.

6. As you become independent from the nest, never put yourself in a financial position where you will have to depend on someone else to take care of you.

7. You become a slave to the system if you go to prison.

8. If you have no work ethic, you will always be broke.

9. If a boy or man puts his hands on you, fight back or let someone know as soon as possible. Never allow a boy or man to get away with hitting you. A man or boy should never put his hands on you—period!

10. The images you see on television, in the movies, on the internet, and in magazines do not define what beauty is. They do not define who you are as a person. You are beautiful just the way you are.

11. Choose your friends wisely. Your friends are a reflection of you.

12. Stay away from makeup as long as possible. You don't need unwanted extra attention.

13. Never walk home or through the neighborhood by yourself.

14. You will have to be ten times as good as those you compete against. You must battle against racism, colorism, sexism, and classism for the rest of your life. Be strong and ready for all challenges.

15. Never disrespect your mother or the women who raised you.

16. Once you push send, you can never get that picture or text message back.

17. Listen more than you speak.

18. Gossip is not cute. Stay out of the girl drama and walk away.

19. Drugs and alcohol: It only takes one hit or one drink to get yourself in trouble.

20. Do not muddy up the family name.

21. Speak boldly and with confidence.
22. Pray and meditate on positive affirmations, daily.
23. You must know how to code switch when needed. (Speech & Movement)
24. If someone has sexually assaulted you, tell someone you trust today.
25. The clothes you put on every day become your uniform. How will your uniform represent who you are out in public?
26. Social media is a drug. It creates the same chemical in the brain (dopamine) that is created when people eat, do drugs, and drink alcohol. Dopamine tells the brain that it needs more of that thing that makes you feel good. The addiction will cause more drama and conflict than you can ever imagine. Stay off of social media as much as possible. Cowards cyberbully others. Not cool! Stop wasting so much time on your phone or computer.
27. Grandma used to tell the young ladies in the neighborhood: *"Ain't nothing out in those streets late at night for you baby girl. The only things open after midnight is gas stations and legs. Listen to me baby, Grandma knows."*
28. This culture of sexual abuse is not just happening in the United States. It's happening in different parts of the world as well. Example: According to the Uganda Violence Against Children Survey 2018, one in three girls ages 18-24 reported experiencing sexual violence during childhood, including 11% of girls experiencing pressured or forced sex (togetherforgirls.org). Please tell someone (you trust) if you or someone you know is being abused. You can stop that person from hurting you and others like you.

Black Girls Rock

Black Girls Rock (www.blackgirlsrockinc.com) is a great movement that encourages and helps girls of color find their voices and build their self-esteem and confidence. Black Girls Rock is a 501(c)3 nonprofit youth empowerment and mentoring organization established to promote the arts for young women of color, as well as to encourage dialogue and analysis of the ways women of color are portrayed in the media. These young ladies have the opportunity to attend camps, think tanks, and conferences. The number of positive tools in the form of volunteers, mentors, social media, books, and the arts are changing lives daily.

Therapy

Some people may not believe in therapy. If you don't, I would say the concept is at least worth doing some research on. I do believe that communicating with other human beings is very important for a healthy human existence. I know for some, insurance can be an issue when it comes to therapy. If you believe therapy works, I suggest looking at your local school. A lot of schools now have social or emotional counselors and other services for students that are free. Every public school in America should have some sort of counselor and psychologist on campus.

Parents, it's worth the effort to at least go to your son's or daughter's school and start asking questions regarding the services that your child can receive. According to the American Psychological Association, an estimated 59 million people have received mental health treatment in the past two years, and 80 percent of them have found it effective therapy. We need outlets to be able to share are pain, our joy, and our dreams. Parents, we need to look for warning signs with our teenagers and get them the help that they need. Teenagers, you must seek the help you need and find someone you trust to help you through whatever issues or fears you may be experiencing. You were born to be great and make a difference on this earth. Find your purpose, and never look back. Don't let the past control your future any longer.

I will embrace my true self. I will let no one define who I am. I will fight for my life for the rest of my life.

~Notes~

27

I'm Not a Salesman

28

I was talking to a good friend of mine who has a brilliant creative mind. He created an incredible educational tool for middle school students. I've seen and read his work firsthand. He is sitting on a million-dollar product.

I was talking to him one day and we started talking about his product. He started showing me his excellent website. As we were talking, he made the comment, "I'm not a salesman. That's not what I do. I want to pitch this to different school districts, but I'm just not a salesman. I'm just not good at it."

I'm not a salesman either if I don't have any passion for the product, but if I have passion for the product and especially if the product is my creation, then I have no problem trying to convince people how good it is. What I want him to understand is that this is his baby. I know he's passionate about what he has created. He has to get over that fear and sell his product to whoever will listen. He has to be his own biggest cheerleader. If he truly wants his educational tool to take off like a wildfire, he's going to have to take the lead on all promotion efforts. The right people will definitely help and invest in his product once they see how passionate he is about it. All 4 Me Books, coming to a young mind near you!

No one should be more excited about our ideas, visions, or finished products than we are. If we're not excited about telling people about our finished creations, how do we expect anyone else to be excited about it?

No one knows our products like we do. No one knows all of the pain and long hours it took to complete our finished masterpiece! No one knows how we deeply and truly feel about the birth of our baby, whatever that baby may be.

Has this ever happened to you? One of your friends starts selling insurance, loans, juice, vitamins, vacations, or whatever the new phase is and convinces you to start selling the product as well. You start doing it because your friend is so excited about it. He or she convinces you of how much money you can make if you just buy into the process. It's happened to me a few times. I was out there trying to sell stuff just to make a few extra bucks because someone talked me into it with his/her excitement for the product. I even sold Mary Kay products at one point. I had a giant tackle box full of lipstick, eyeliner, blush, masks, and scrubs—you name it, and I had it. I would even make gift baskets during the holidays. One night when I was in my late twenties, I even put myself in danger for Mary Kay's dream.

Mary Kay in the Hood

Warning: I'm about to code switch, so you are going to read a lot of slang in this passage.

So, in true Mary Kay fashion, I locked down an appointment with a client. I drove to a client's home one particular night to give my exciting presentation. Number one, I drove into the middle of the hood in south central Los Angeles. But hey, I was trying my best to make a dollar out of fifteen cents.

So, I parked my car in this non-desirable neighborhood and walked up to my client's front door and rang the doorbell. When the door opened, a man came to the door around my age. I was twenty-six at the time. The guy had on a wife-beater, sagging pants, tattoos, and cornrows in his hair.

I said, "What's going on, bruh? I'm a Mary Kay consultant, and I have an appointment with (we'll just call her Tanya)."

He looked me up and down like he was about to fire on me. I was thinking to myself, *What the hell? Oh boy is tripping. I might have to drop this box and get a few off before this fool tries to rush me.*

He didn't say anything to me. He just turned around and started yelling at his baby mama. "Oh, so you got this niggah all up in here around my daughter? You got busters all up in here whenever you want, huh? You better get this fool up out of here before I put a cap in his a——!"

She says, "Look, you need to get out of my house. You really need to leave, coming up in here with all this drama."

Like a fool, I'm still standing at the door, listening to all this madness. I was just about to walk back to my car before she came to the door. "Don't worry about him. He's just tripping. That's my daughter's father. I am so sorry. He was just leaving." She gave him this look like, "Don't make me slap the hell out of you!"

He came to the door and walked past me, looking disgusted. I'm standing there in disbelief. The street side of me was thinking, *I ain't no punk! This fool better recognize! We can do this if need be!* The educated and rational side of me was thinking, *This fool is crazy! Let me get up out of here, before I'm on the six o'clock news.*

To make things even worse, after he left, I did my one-hour presentation. I showed her how to put on our cleansing mask and gave great information on different shades of lipsticks and eyeliners that were perfect for her complexion. When it was all said and done, she spent a whopping ten dollars. What?! You mean to tell me I almost went to jail or the hospital for ten dollars?! What a night! Every time I see a pink car, I just laugh to myself.

Anyway, I would make anywhere from two hundred to five hundred dollars a week, but it was not my passion. I was selling someone else's dream because Mary Kay's representative was super excited about the product. I believe this is how excited we need to be about our own products that we create with our own minds, hands, and hard work.

We have to stop making other people rich and start investing in our own visions and dreams. Let's get excited about our own passions, and let the world experience our great creations. Our mouths should always be the loudest and most informative about our own products.

I would suggest taking a speech communications and marketing class that will help you gain more confidence in your sales skills. Also, here's a great book to consider if you really want the world to know about your creation:

- *Building a Story Brand* by Donald Miller
  This book will help you explore a variety of topics, like:
- ❖ What's your message?
- ❖ Can you say it easily?
- ❖ Is it simple, relevant, and repeatable?
- ❖ Why so many businesses fail
- ❖ Clear communication
- ❖ Storytelling
- ❖ Keep it simple

> *No one should be able to push your idea, your dream,*
> *your vision, or your product like you can.*
>
> ~ Donald Miller

~Notes~

28

_____
_____
_____
_____
_____
_____
_____
_____
_____
_____
_____
_____
_____
_____
_____
_____
_____
_____
_____
_____
_____

I'm Not Smart Enough

29

Simple solution: start reading! We all know that not only do we have books, magazines, and papers. We have more information at our fingertips now than any other time in history. The internet has transformed the access to informational databases in ways we could've never imagined. There are so many apps out there, you can't count them all. It's simply amazing how with one click of a button, you can learn about whatever you want.

"I'm not smart enough" should never be the reason why we are not accomplishing our goals. If you don't understand it the first time, read it again, and then read it again and again and again until you get it. Ask questions about the new information you've learned. Talk to those in the field who have experience. Put your new knowledge base into action.

If a lot of us would stop using our phones and computers for just social media purposes, we could actually learn a lot about whatever it is we are ignorant about. We can even get second, third, and forth opinions on whatever article we read. Hopefully, the more information we gather, the better decisions we'll be able to make regarding what's important to us.

YouTube instructional videos are golden. Those instructional videos have saved me so much money over the years, it's ridiculous. The motivational videos are phenomenal as well. I listen to people like Les Brown, Tony Robbins Dr. Eric Thomas, Will Smith, C.T. Fletcher, T. D. Jakes, Ray Lewis, Kobe Bryant, Kendrick Lamar, Jay Z, Oprah Winfrey,

Terry Crews, and many more. I try to start every morning with some type of motivational message to get my mind jump-started for the day. Technology can be amazing to our mental, spiritual, and financial future if we use this superpower wisely.

God has given us all of the mental tools we need to consciously be as informed and as successful as we want to be. It's up to us how we use those tools. Of course, some of us do not pick things up as fast as others, but that's okay. Just be patient; it will come to you if you keep reading, keep asking questions, and keep applying the information that helps you move in the direction you want to go. If you develop a passion for that knowledge and turn that knowledge into action, it will guide you to places that you would've never imagined.

Seminars, conferences, and webinars are also great ways to gather the information we need that will take us to the next level of obtaining our goals. One minute we're ignorant about the information that we want, and the next minute we're not. We have to invest in ourselves first if we want big results in our own lives. We must surround ourselves with people and information that is going to support our belief systems.

Real Estate?

When I was twenty-seven years old, I knew nothing about real estate. I learned a few years prior that my cousin was buying rental properties left and right. He had about fifteen or twenty rental properties all over the country. For whatever reason I never thought to ask him how he was able to afford all of those houses. So, one day when I was at his house, he and a friend were talking about taking a trip to Arizona to look at rental properties. I became excited instantly! Flying to another state and buying property really fascinated me.

I just simply asked him could I go with them on the trip. After they said yes, I then started to ask more questions. How did you find out about these houses in Arizona? How do you generate money to afford these house? How do you make real money from owning rental properties? All of these questions were swirling through my head.

The first thing he told me was that they learned about these type of investment properties when they go to a particular seminar once a month. These seminars were conducted by the Marshall Reddick Real Estate group. It was a free seminar with loads of real estate information and great opportunities to invest in properties all over the United States. It sounded good to me, so I was all in. I went to my first meeting and I was hooked. I did not know anything about the real estate game until I started going to these seminars. I learned about property management. I learned about refinancing. I learned about different types of loans and how different markets appreciate. I learned so much in a short amount of time.

Within two years, I was able to purchase four houses across the country because of the information I had obtained. I had to change my mind-set from doing what I've always done to doing what I had never done before and trusting the process. This entire process taught me if I didn't have the information I needed, it was my responsibility to go out and get it.

After four years, I did notice a flaw in my strategy though. I let my emotions get the best of me. I came to the realization that I purchased too many houses without enough reserves in the bank. I became greedy. For those not familiar with owning rental properties; For every house you buy, you need at least $15,000 of reserves in savings for the upkeep of your properties and extra expenses. You must always take in account the damage created by bad renters, getting the property rent-ready, property management fees, and properties with no renters.

My problem was that I only had $15,000 in the bank to manage my four rental properties. It was not enough to keep up with the upkeep, vacant rentals, and the changing market that hit in 2008. I had to sell my homes, but I learned a lot in the process. By the grace of God, four years later, I was put in a position to start over again and buy another home.

I can confidently say now, no matter the setback, I will always lean toward real estate when it comes to investing. Over the years, I've learned a ton, and I know for sure that I will never make the same mistakes I made in my early thirties.

The truth for a lot of us, is that we don't like change. We want to keep doing things the way we've always done them. We get lazy in our thinking and refuse to adapt to our changing environments. If we keep this mentality, the world just passes us by and we continue using the excuse, "I'm not smart enough." Our eyes and minds will remain wide shut or they will slowly open so we can eventually see and go get what it is we truly want.

If we always do what we've always done, we will
always get what we've always got.

~ Henry Ford

~Notes~

29

I Don't Have Any
Time to Work Out

30

It all comes down to your priorities. Is your body a priority to you? Let me ask you another question. How many extra bodies do you have in your closet? If I had to predict your answer, I would bet my house that you said *none*. This is it! We only get one body in our lifetime. If we don't take care of it now, it won't take care of us later. Many of us tend to make time for everything and everyone else but ourselves. In my opinion, no one, not your kids, your spouse, your significant other, your siblings, your parents, or your friends, should ever come before your health. You're good to no one if you don't have good health.

We have to take time for ourselves. It's a must! Whatever it is that helps you relieve stress, helps you strengthen muscles, helps you with aerobic endurance, or helps you release endorphins, this is exactly the activity that you need to take time for. Working out three days a week will definitely get you started in the right direction. You may have to get up at three o'clock in the morning to get it done, or you may have to get it done at nine o'clock at night. Whatever you have to do to make working out a part of your life, just do it.

I think most people would agree that working out, eating healthy food, and consistently keeping junk food and pollutants out of our bodies will help us feel mentally and physically ready to attack each day. Listen, I've seen the man who helped raise me go from 140 pounds all the way down to 70 pounds. Smoking cigarettes and drinking alcohol slowing destroyed his body until he passed away. He was a good man, but his body just could not take the abuse any longer. He was only seventy years young when he left us.

I have an older brother who is a black belt in karate and used to look like a lightweight bodybuilder when he was in his late twenties and thirties. At sixty-three years old, he now weighs anywhere between 120 and 130 pounds. He's been drinking and smoking for years. Unfortunately, all of those years of drinking and smoking caught up with him. He slowly started losing blood circulation in his left foot and leg. His leg got so bad that eventually his foot turned as black a Raiders jersey. After a few days at the hospital in excruciating pain, the doctors finally walked into his room and told him that the foot could not be saved. It was so bad, they had to cut right below the knee so they could get all of the affected area.

I mentioned these two family members because I wanted you to know that I've seen firsthand how the body can slowly and quickly deteriorate when it's not taken care of properly. Our bodies literally depend on physical activity and less intake of toxins and edible pollution to function at their best each and every day.

Working out at home may be your best option if you can't get to the gym, park, yoga class, pool, or track on a consistent basis. Check this out: Research shows that if you do something for twenty-one days, that something will become a habit. If you can stay consistent and mentally focused, your mind will automatically push your body to get up, get out, and get going.

Create a Plan

The one essential thing that helps me stay organized is writing out a schedule for the next day. I literally write out my expectations for the following day. My schedule always changes according to my work schedule. Here is an example of what I wrote last night. As I'm writing this chapter, I am currently on vacation.

4–4:30 a.m. – Pray and meditate

4:30–4:45 a.m. – Take Phoenix and Ghost (our dogs) out for their walk and feed them

5–5:30 a.m. – Eat and surf CNN and Yahoo

6–7 a.m. – Gym

7:30–8:00 a.m. – Shower

8:30–11:30 a.m. – Write (work on book)

12–1 p.m. – Golf range

2–4 p.m. – Get tattoo

4:30–6 p.m. – Eat/relax

7–10 p.m. – Family time

I know this maybe too extreme for some people. But hey, it's just an example. Of course, you can always use the calendar in your phone to help organize your busy days. You can just write the must-do items. Here's a generic example:

Sunday	Monday	Tuesday	Wednesday	Thursday	Friday	Saturday
1 Mountain hike 8 a.m. –1 p.m.	2 Bikram yoga 6–8 p.m.	3 Gym 5–6 a.m. Practice 2:15–4 p.m.	4 Bikram yoga 6–8 p.m.	5 Gym 5–6 a.m. Practice 2:15–4 p.m.	6 John's football game 7:30 p.m.	7 Golf practice 6:30 a.m.– 12 p.m.
8 Church 8–9:30 a.m. Bowling 10 a.m. –12 p.m.	9 Project 3–5 a.m. Bikram yoga 6–8 p.m.	10 Gym 5–6 a.m. Therapy 6–7 p.m.	11 Staff meeting 2–3 p.m. Bikram yoga 6–8 p.m.	12 Gym 5–6 a.m.	13 Project 3–5 a.m. Bikram yoga 6–8 p.m.	14
15 Church 8–9:30 a.m.	16 Gym 5–6 a.m.	17 Pick up John from practice 7 p.m.	18	19 Pick up John from practice 7 p.m.	20 John's football game 7:30 p.m.	21

22	23	24	25	26	27	28
Bowling 10 a.m.–12 p.m.	Gym 5–6 a.m.	Bikram yoga 6–8 p.m.		Swing coach 3:30–4:30 p.m. Bikram yoga 6–8 p.m.		

29	30	31
Golf 8 a.m.–2 p.m.	Gym 5–6 a.m.	Yoga 6–8 p.m.

Make sure you set an alert in your cell phone or computer to remind you of your events and workouts that are important to you. I know that sounds obvious when you repeat it to yourself, but some of us may not know that.

Start Small

If you only have five to ten minutes a day, take those minutes to work out. Something is better than nothing. Do push-ups, sit-ups, lunges, curls, or pull-ups or take a walk—just *do something*. Those minutes will slowly start to increase over time as the endorphins in your body start to give you more and more energy.

Watch and Work

While you're watching television, you can get some work in. Keep workout bands, dumbbells, rollers, sliders, and maybe even a jump rope in the television area. Keep a deck of cards nearby as well. I got the deck of cards idea from Ray Lewis (retired Baltimore Ravens Super Bowl champion). He tells an amazing short story about part of his life on YouTube titled "52 Cards." It's a great motivational speech. Dr. Thomas's words of wisdom are sprinkled in this message as well.

So, you take a deck of cards and turn them facedown. When you flip a card over, look at the number and do that number of push-ups, sit-ups, lunges, burpees, speed jump squats, or whatever your working on. Face cards are worth ten, aces twenty-five, and jokers fifty. You can start off with ten cards, or you can go through the entire deck. It's a fun way to mix up your workout, while you're in front of the television.

Workout videos are great as well. Here are few I would suggest. Take a deeper look at these quality videos by visiting www.beachbody.com. Also, make sure you check with your physician before you start any new program.

- P90X (incredible, worked very well for me)
- P90X3
- P90
- Insanity
- Insanity Max:30
- Double Time
- Clean Week
- Shift Shop
- YOUv2
- Country Heat
- PiYO
- 21 Day Fix
- Core De Force
- 3 Week Yoga Retreat
- Cize
- Tai Cheng
- Focus T25
- Body Beast

Home Workout Systems

- Peloton (www.onepeloton.com)
- Mirror (www.mirror.com)

Community Websites That May Interest You

- www.fitlinksystems.com

This is a great community fitness site. This site has great tools to get you in shape and connect you with others. It has recent exercises by Fitlink members to give you some direction. You can type in what city you're in and what activity you want to do, and it will give you the information you need that is near your location. The site also allows you to research personal trainers in your area and find classes and fitness events you might be interested in.

- ibodyfit.com
- fit4mom.com (for people with kids ages one to five)
- Bikram yoga or Hot Yoga (105 degrees. Find a Studio in your city.) Bikram yoga is a ninety-minute class of twenty-six postures. The class is great for releasing impurities from the body. It is therapeutic for strengthening and stretching the muscles, organs, and glands in the body. Bikram and Hot Yoga classes are located in most cities in the United States. Search the internet for a studio near you.

Delegate

You can definitely free up some time in your schedule if responsibility around the house is delegated. Everyone should have some responsibility of doing chores around the house. No one should do all of the work or chores. If you live by yourself, you might want to hire a cleaning service a few days out of the month to free up some time. Can't afford it? Try the neighbors' teenagers. They'll work for cheap. Can't afford that? Don't want anyone in your space? Well, you're simply going to have to get up earlier to get things done if you're serious about freeing up time for yourself and your health.

Prepare for the Next Day

If you are working out in the morning, lay out your workout clothes the night before. If you're working out in the evening, put your workout clothes in your gym bag and put it by the door or put it in your car the night before.

Athletes ~ Middle School ~ High School ~ College

If you don't have any time to work out away from practice, you will never reach your full potential. Athletes who are less talented than you will pass you by at a rapid rate. Coaches don't have the time to work with all of their athletes individually on their weaknesses. That is your job. You must do that on your own. When you see athletes like Kobe Bryant, Steph Curry, Michael Jordan, Tom Brady, Russel Wilson, Tiger Woods, Dustin Johnson, Serena and Venus Williams, LeBron James, Shaun White, Tiger Woods, and Michael Phelps winning and doing incredible things on game day, that is the essence of hours, days, months, and years of sweat, blood, tears, repetitions, bleachers, laps, weight training, film, injuries, ice baths, and minimal sleep. All of this hard work is done behind the scenes and away from a regular routine practice day.

Write a schedule. Put it in your phone. Stop reading your press clippings. Stop listening to your friends and family telling you how good you are. Stop missing workouts. Stop missing practice and get it done. I guarantee you that your competition is grinding and trying to take your spot while you're taking a break. If you want to be great, you have to find the time to create greatness. We all the same 24hrs.

The only time success comes before work is in the dictionary.
One body, one mind, one life is all we get.

~Notes~

30

College and Professional Development Schools Are Just Too Expensive

High School Graduates and Everyone Else Who's Out of School

31

You are absolutely right! They are too expensive. I wish it were free. No matter what college you want to go to:—nail college; hair and makeup school; acting school; real estate school; Hamburger University; Phoenix University; DeVry; University of California, Irvine; New York University; University of Miami; California State University, Long Beach State; Pepperdine University; University of Nevada, Reno; Stanford University; University of California, Los Angeles; or Harvard—it's going to cost some money that you (most likely) don't have. If you're saying college or any post high school course is too expensive, you are saying what every high school, college, and career student has been saying since the beginning of time. The question you have to ask yourself is this: Do my ideas, work ethic, and passion need to take a journey through one of these institutions for my dreams to become a reality?

If the answer is yes, then you have to find a way to get yourself into somebody's school! Here are two worst-case scenarios. Scenario #1: You never realize your true potential and continue to do what you're doing for the rest of your life. Scenario #2: You take out a student loan. That's it. Most of us who took out student loans didn't want to do it, but we knew it had to be done for our journeys to continue. What more is there to say?

Here are a few resources that will help you with your mission, if you choose to accept it:

Scholarships

- ❖ www.scholarhips.com
- ❖ www.studentscholarshipsearch.com
- ❖ www.cheapscholar.org (Last name Gatlin(g): get $18,000 per year at North Carolina State)
- ❖ www.nitrocollege.com (minority scholarships)

Financial Aid

- ❖ www.fafsa.ed.gov
- ❖ www.finaid.org
- ❖ www.empire.edu (Beauty School)
- ❖ www.hairacademymd.com
- ❖ www.bellusacademy.edu
- ❖ www.nyfa.edu
- ❖ www.disneydreamersacademy.com
- ❖ www.mcdonalds.com
- ❖ www.aada.edu
- ❖ www.actingstudio.com
- ❖ www.nursing.emory.edu
- ❖ www.westcoastuniversity.edu

My future is a click away.

~Notes~

31

_____
_____
_____
_____
_____
_____
_____
_____
_____
_____
_____
_____
_____
_____
_____
_____
_____
_____
_____
_____
_____
_____

Someone Else Is Already Doing It

32

Right again. Someone has already written a book on the same subject, but that person didn't let the competition scare him or her away. Instead, they rose to the challenge and fought for their passion and vision. What will you do to stand tall among giants? How will you or your product be relevant to the rest of the world?

Let me share with you a few small lists of companies or brands that are doing the same thing; but they all have their own personal stamp on what they do. They all started small, and now they're all giants in their industries.

Shoes

- Nike
- Adidas
- Converse
- Sketchers
- Puma
- Air Jordan's
- New Balance

- K-Swiss
- Under Armour

Cars and Trucks

- Mercedes Benz
- BMW
- Jaguar
- Lexus
- Volvo
- Chrysler
- Ford
- Toyota
- GMC

Actors

- Denzel Washington
- Bradley Cooper
- Leonardo DiCaprio
- Tom Cruise
- Will Smith
- The Rock
- Vin Diesel
- Jim Carrey
- Johnny Depp
- Al Pacino
- Robert De Niro
- Brad Pitt

Golf Equipment

- Adams
- Cobra
- Mizuno
- Cleveland
- Bridgestone

- Ping
- Callaway
- TaylorMade
- Titleist

Professional Athletes

- Steph Curry
- Kobe Bryant (R.I.P #8 ~ #24)
- LeBron James
- Jerry Rice
- Odell Beckham Jr.
- Randy Moss
- Venus Williams
- Serena Williams
- Clayton Kershaw
- Matt Kemp
- Yasiel Puig
- Phil Mickelson
- Tiger Woods

Restaurants

- McDonald's
- Burger King
- Jack in the Box
- Denny's
- Cheesecake Factory
- Houston's
- Five Guys
- Toppers Pizza
- Taco Bell
- Sharky's
- Pizza Hut
- Domino's Pizza

If I had the time, I could probably give you a thousand lists of people and companies that are doing the exact same thing, and they're all making an exclusive path for themselves and their clients. How are you going to be exclusive and relevant, regardless of how many other brands like yours are out there? What does your brand have that the others don't? What's special about you? Once you figure that out, your future clients will notice as well, and you will reap the benefits. Do me a favor. Create your own list and put your brand at the top of that list. Write down your short- and long-term goals and get to work. This is what you were born to do! Now, go out and make it happen!

I'm going to mention this amazing resource for a second time.

- *Building a Story Brand* by Donald Miller
  - ❖ What's your message?
  - ❖ Can you say it easily?
  - ❖ Is it simple, relevant, and repeatable?
  - ❖ Why so my businesses fail
  - ❖ Clear communication
  - ❖ Storytelling
  - ❖ Keep it simple

Do what you do better than anyone else!

~Notes~

32

I'm Not Motivated Enough

33

You're absolutely right.! If you're not motivated, nothing will change in your life. Find something that you think and dream about every day. If it means something to you and you truly care about it, the motivation to act will come naturally. Do whatever you need to do to get yourself jump-started. Search day and night for your gift or gifts. The reality is, you don't have to search very far because your gifts are already inside of you. You just need someone to help you pull them out and develop them. Usually, gifts are things that come naturally easy for us. Once we find our gift or gifts, we must develop them to a point where they become second nature, and we become excellent at our chosen craft.

There are plenty of motivational videos on YouTube to watch and listen to. Maybe you just need to talk to someone in your potential area of interest. Talk to someone you trust in your family. They may know what your gift is before you do. Talk to a mentor, a teacher, a coach, or maybe your pastor has a few words of encouragement and insight.

Once you get that spark, you have to keep the flame burning with your actions. Consistent commitment is the only thing that will change our finances, our bodies, our relationships, our projects, our grades, our team status, or our promotion status. No one can want what we want more than us.

Some people don't want much, so they don't get much.

~Notes~
33

I Can't Handle Failure

34

Failure (noun): Lack of success, nonfulfillment, frustration, defeat, collapse, misfiring, coming to nothing.

Failure is always going to be a part of life. Let's look at baseball for a quick second. In baseball, if you hit the ball and get on base three out of every ten times at bat, you're considered to be a good hitter. In other words, if you strike out seven out of ten times at bat, you're considered to be a consistent and reliable batter.

In major league baseball, that means you're one of the best. These players embrace failure, and they know greatness is waiting for them if they stay focused and committed. They know if they start pouting and feeling sorry for themselves, nothing will change. Their confidence level in their ability is so high, they actually believe that the failure they experience is only temporary.

Top 10 MLB Ranked Players in 2019 (Source: ESPN Statistics)

Player	Team	Batting Average & OBP
Josh Bell	Pittsburgh Pirates	.333–.402
George Springer	Houston Astros	.318–.402
Cody Bellinger	Los Angeles Dodgers	.409–.487
Christian Yelich	Milwaukee Brewers	.32–.444

Marcell Ozuna	St. Louis Cardinals	.226–.309
Domingo Santana	Seattle Mariners	.269–.340
Adalberto Mondesi	Kansas City Royals	.276–.313
Jose Abreu	Chicago White Sox	.260–.321
Rhys Hoskins	Philadelphia Phillies	.267–.390
Nolan Arenado	Colorado Rockies	.313–.361

Here's the truth: We are going to fail way more than we succeed in this life. You might get a hundred No's before you get that one yes that changes your life. As crazy as it may sound, we have to keep coming back for more and more rejection, especially when the odds are not in our favor.

If we can't handle failure, we will never succeed or sustain success for any long period of time. We will always be frustrated and continue to tear down our progress. I understand pushing yourself hard and being your own biggest critic, but it shouldn't be to the point where you are constantly doubting yourself and getting in your own way. Whining and crying every time you make a mistake will never make you better at what you're trying to accomplish.

We have to learn how to learn from our own mistakes. Mistakes and bad decisions are meant to teach us something about ourselves and our current situations. If we continue to make the same mistakes over and over expecting different results, we can only chalk those experiences up to small fits of insanity.

Don't go through life running from your failures. Use them as fuel to move forward with confidence. Your failures should build layer after layer of thick skin and resilience. Failure hurts, but it will make you stronger to fail again, conquer, fail again, conquer, and fail again, day after day, month after month, or year after year. Embrace your failures and make them your best allies. They will help you if you let them. They will push you if you allow them to. I heard Will Smith say this in an interview one night: "You can't win the war against the world, if you can't win the war against your own mind."

Success is not final. Failure is not fatal; it is the
courage to continue that counts.

~ Winston Churchill

~Notes~

34

_____
_____
_____
_____
_____
_____
_____
_____
_____
_____
_____
_____
_____
_____
_____
_____
_____
_____
_____
_____
_____

I'm Not Ready

35

Sometimes you just have to step in, step up, and show out. The only way to truly get ready is to throw yourself into the process. You have to commit to the process and commit and learn as you go. You can't be afraid to make mistakes, and you can't be afraid to fail.

If you need a little comfort and guidance, make sure you find a mentor you can trust. You need someone who understands your journey and your struggle. You need someone who will tell you the truth about yourself and the decisions you've made or are thinking about making. You also need that person you can truly trust with your frustrations, when you really need to vent and complain. We will explore more about mentors in chapter 38.

Nevada Wolfpack versus Southern Illinois ~ Football Game ~ September 2, 1989

I had just turned eighteen years old two months prior to this game. This was the first game of the season during my freshman year. As a true freshman, I had successfully won the backup role to the starting quarterback. So, the first game of my college career was underway. Surprisingly, by the end of the first quarter, our starting quarterback had already thrown one interception, and our offense was not moving the ball successfully at all. To my surprise, our head coach, Coach Ault, threw me to the wolves after our offense stalled again in the second quarter. Imagine being eighteen years old and running into your first college football game with twenty thousand screaming fans. I was excited and scared all at the same time. Was I completely ready? Uhhh, no! I definitely was not fully ready, but I was somewhat prepared, and my number was called. It was time to step up and stand out or humiliate myself and the team. No pressure though. Once I got in the game, I had to get mentally ready very quickly.

My teammates, coaches, and fans were expecting this eighteen-year-old freshman to lead these twenty, twenty-one-, and twenty-two-year-old men to victory. I was so nervous, I kept forgetting to look at the defensive coverage during my first series of plays. Every time I came to the sideline during the first series, Coach Ault would ask me the coverage, and I seriously had no clue. The only thing I was worried about was getting hit and getting the play off before the play clock reached zero.

But the more I played, the more the speed of the game slowed down. I slowly started recognizing coverages and using the God-given talents that helped me get the scholarship in the first place. With God on my side, by the end of the half, I had managed to throw three touchdowns to start my college career. The crowd was electrifying, and my confidence grew more and more with every completion and every touchdown. We ended up winning the game 41–3, and my confidence and belief in myself exploded to another level. The most important lesson I learned on that day, was that I must always be willing and courageous enough to step into unchartered waters when I least expect to do so.

We may not have all of the answers or know exactly what we're doing, but if we stay the course, the experience alone will teach us more than we could ever imagine. The best way to grow is by taking risks, learning from the good and the bad, and embracing both.

Marcos Alonso, author of the article "You Will Never Be Ready. Do It Anyway!," makes a great point when he says, "Opportunities force us to take one more step, to reinvent ourselves, to run into the unknown and to leave the comfort zone in which we are used to living."

From Assistant Principal to Principal

Was I 100 percent ready to step into the principal role at my school? No, sir. No, ma'am. I didn't even know the position was coming my way until our principal at the time was promoted to the district office. One day I was an assistant principal, and a few weeks later, I was appointed the principal intern. It took some guts to be able to step into that position, especially at the same school with the same staff.

You notice very quickly that your previous relationships with staff members change, and people either have more or less respect for you, depending on their perception of you. I had to learn how to lead certain staff members who didn't necessarily understand the concepts of team and family. Coming from a sports background, that's all I know. "I've got your back. I'm going to help you because you are my teammate." This is the philosophy that was ingrained in me since I was twelve years old. That's all I've ever known. When working with youth, I only have one exception. If your actions are harming and abusing the mental and physical well- being of the child, then I must do all I can do to protect that child.

I quickly had to learn that not everyone understands or even believes in the team philosophy. For some, it's always been teachers versus administration. So, I had to regroup and refocus. I also had to study, delegate, and learn how to multitask on steroids compared to when I was an AP (assistant principal). I definitely had to endure a few bumps and bruises when my journey first began. I had to learn how to take the punches of mistakes and criticism (known and unknown), keep my sanity, and not let the people or the job swallow me up and spit me out.

As a principal, you quickly realize that certain staff members have their own agendas and they tend to push their problems on you at the most hectic times of the day or week. I've learned as a leader that my problems come second, and my staff's come first. It is what it is. Some staff members just don't realize all of the responsibilities that a principal has on a daily basis, or they simply choose not to think about it. So, let me share a few:

- ❖ Teacher complaints about students
- ❖ Student complaints about teachers
- ❖ Parent complaints about teachers

- ❖ Parent conferences
- ❖ Missing students
- ❖ Staff complaints about other staff members
- ❖ Conference summaries
- ❖ Warning letters
- ❖ Letters of reprimand
- ❖ Parents fighting parents in the neighborhood
- ❖ Adults fighting students
- ❖ Budget
- ❖ Staff members abusing their authority
- ❖ Mandated Reporting
- ❖ Master schedule
- ❖ Staff meetings
- ❖ Creating staff meeting agendas
- ❖ Running staff meetings
- ❖ Leadership meetings
- ❖ School site council meetings
- ❖ Coffee with the principal
- ❖ Creating staff binders
- ❖ Sports programs
- ❖ Dances
- ❖ Field trips
- ❖ Campus supervisor evaluations
- ❖ Security evaluations
- ❖ Teacher evaluations
- ❖ Classroom observations
- ❖ Classified evaluations
- ❖ Principal meetings
- ❖ Board presentations
- ❖ Board meetings
- ❖ Special education issues
- ❖ Suicide assessments
- ❖ Threat assessments
- ❖ Lunchtime supervision
- ❖ Restorative justice circles
- ❖ Scheduling

- ❖ IEP meetings
- ❖ Before and after school supervision

Just wanted to mention a few.

Trust me when I say trusting and listening to my leadership team my first year, proved to be my best offense and defense against the daily full-court press of running a school.

Every time I stepped through the front door of my school, I definitely learned something new about myself, the job, managing my time, and managing people. One thing I learned quickly is that the word *no* is definitely a great word to have in your vocabulary as a principal and leader of men and women. I've also learned very quickly that people will try their best to take your kindness for weakness. If you allow unacceptable behavior to continue, it will become the culture and not the exception.

Whether you're still learning the job, learning the program, or learning the plays, you must stay the course if you want to get better at what you do. You can eventually master what you do if you do it long enough, study the job, study your position, read, and listen to a mentor. One of the most important lessons I learned my first year was you must humble yourself, learn from others, embrace your mistakes, and be willing to adjust and call an audible at the drop of a hat.

Ready or not, be ready to step up, show up and show out. It's your time.

~Notes~

35

_____
_____
_____
_____
_____
_____
_____
_____
_____
_____
_____
_____
_____
_____
_____
_____
_____
_____
_____
_____
_____
_____
_____
_____

I Don't Have Time to Pray or Meditate

36

Prayer (verb): A solemn request for help or expression of thanks addressed to God, a higher power, or an object of worship.

I don't know if you believe in God, Jesus, Buddha, Allah, or some other higher power. But I do know that whatever you believe in, it only takes a few minutes or even a few seconds to pray. When we pray, we are consciously giving all of our power over to another source that we believe is bigger and more powerful than we are. When we pray, we are either asking for help, asking for forgiveness, or being thankful for what we have. We humble ourselves to the realization that we cannot do anything without the help and guidance of our higher power.

Some people like to pray on their knees, while others like to pray standing up or sitting down. Some people even pray while their walking, lying in bed, driving to work, or playing in a sporting event or competition. Wherever and whenever we pray, it only takes a moment of our time. I believe my God is more interested in the quality of my prayers rather than the quantity. In my opinion, short, sincere, and meaningful prayers are more heartfelt than long, drawn-out, selfish ones. Don't get me wrong. There is nothing wrong with long prayers. We just need to make sure that our prayers are coming from a good place.

Simple Prayers

- Thank you.
- Grant me the serenity to accept the things I cannot change, courage to change the things I can, and the wisdom to know the difference.
- Please forgive me of my sins.
- Lord, help me not lean on my own understanding, but in everything acknowledge you so that you can direct my words, thoughts, and actions.
- Help me.
- Thank you for providing me with my health, food, and a roof over my head.
- Thank you for sending people to help me.
- Give that family strength.
- Give me strength to overcome this challenge that I face.
- I believe that you are my Lord and personal savior.
- Your word says, "If you declare with your mouth, 'Jesus is Lord,' and believe in your heart that God raised him from the dead, you will be saved." I believe.
- Please anoint the doctors' and nurses' hands.
- Please anoint the engine, instruments, wings, and the pilot's mind as we fly to our destination.
- Please send people into my life who can help me be a better and more productive person.
- I don't understand why this happened, but please show me what I need to do. Show me a path that leads to strength and peace. Show me the gifts I need to take from this.
- Help my son/daughter. Send anyone who can help.
- Thank you for my job.
- Thank you for this gift. Please help me move toward the right mind-set, so I can develop it.
- Thank you for another day to be of service.
- Please guide me, so I can lead my family (my team, my employees) in the direction we need to go.
- Save me.

- Please help me forgive those who have hurt me. The pain that I feel, may it not control my actions. Help me understand that it is my responsibility to take my power back.
- Temptations are all around me. Help me keep my mind focused in times of weakness.

Hopefully, these simple prayers will help you or someone you know. There are millions of prayers, but these are just a few that my higher power (God) placed on my heart to share with you.

Meditation/Positive Affirmations

Meditation: A practice where an individual uses a technique, such as mindfulness or focusing his or her mind on a particular object, thought, or activity, to train attention and awareness. To achieve a mentally clear and emotionally calm and stable state of mind.

Many of us may think of meditation as being in a room by yourself or full of people, closing your eyes, and chatting sounds that have no meaning. Well, the meditation I'm talking about is far from that. This meditation is very powerful, meaningful, and life-changing.

The Zone

I learned this form of meditation from a sports psychologist when I was in college. It all started after a game I had. During this particular game, I literally could do no wrong. I completed pass after pass, touchdown after touchdown. Nothing phased me. I was so focused I could barely hear the crowd when I was playing. I remember some of my teammates asking me, "How are you so calm right now?" I couldn't explain it, but I knew deep down in my core that I could not be stopped. I was able to slow the game down to a point where the defense looked like they were moving in slow motion. Some people call this state of being the *zone.*

Up until this point, I had only heard about the zone from professional athletes on television such as Michael Jordan, Magic Johnson, Joe Montana, Steve Young, and Sugar Ray Leonard. After that game, I sat at my locker pondering what had just happened. I thought about the zone, and I definitely knew at that moment, I was just in it. I thought to myself, *I want to experience this over and over again.*

So, during the next few weeks, I did a little research and found a sports psychologist in downtown Reno. My question to him was this: Does the zone just come and go whenever it wants, or is it something you can control and master? He explained to me that the zone is something you can create whenever you want. That's all I needed to hear, so we got started on this journey right away.

He took me into one of his rooms at his office and told me to lie on my back. He turned off the lights and told me to close my eyes. He put on a tape of positive sports affirmations and told me to repeat them quietly to myself one after another. The voice on the tape was very calming as the affirmations were spoken over very tranquil music. He told me to imagine myself doing everything that the affirmations suggested. He told me, *you want to hypnotize your mind to the point where you start to see those powerful actions happening on the field; You want to train your mind in such a way that your subconscious starts to control your body, and your body starts to do what your subconscious believes to be true.*

As the tapes would come to an end, each tape would end the session by asking me to count down from ten to one. The goal was to stop at a number that represented where I wanted my energy level to be for the rest of the day. Once I got to that number, the command for myself was to open my eyes, and at that point, the meditation session would be complete for the day.

I only had four sessions before he sent me out on my own with a few tapes. The goal was for me to say these affirmations every day and eventually start creating personal affirmations of my own. The more I said them and the more I saw these things happening in my mind, the more I started to believe I could make those things happen. Once I started to believe it, the affirmations became part of my mind-set. The affirmations started to become reality in my mind, and I started acting them out in real life, in real games. I got to a point where I started meditating every weekend before games. I would visualize the game before the game as I walked the field during my pregame routine. I was able to see myself throwing touchdowns, scrambling out of trouble, and playing at my best when my best was needed.

I quickly figured out that the zone was not some elusive magic act that I could only catch every so often. It was something I could create before each and every game. I quickly realized that I had everything I needed to control my mind and body on every given day. I also learned that you must be consistent and mentally strong to enter the zone when you need it most. You think about nothing but execution. You also must be able to block out as much negative energy and stress in your life as possible, when trying to create your zone.

I mentioned all of that to say that meditation is powerful, and it works for me when I consistently use it. I'm able to block out the things in my life that are trying to hold me back. After I stopped playing, I stopped meditating for a while, but later on in my life, I finally realized that meditation should be an everyday thing that is constant in my life. I thought to myself, if it worked for games, it would definitely work in my everyday life. Now, my goal each day is to live in the zone. My goal is to get up every morning and meditate on positive affirmations that will propel me into amazingly productive days. I go to my quiet place in the house and turn off the lights, so I will not have any interruptions. When I'm done, I count down from ten to one and stop at the number that will represent my energy level for the day. When I meditate on positive affirmations, my days turn out much better than the days I don't. Life tries its best to interrupt this zone process and take me back to an average, emotional, and inconsistent mind-set.

Affirmations That Work for Me

- No weapon formed against me shall prosper today.
- I am a good man.
- I am intelligent.
- Today is going to be a great day.
- I will handle adversity with class and dignity today.
- I am a good leader.
- I am a millionaire.
- My presentation will be flawless.
- Today I will be a good listener.

- I will finish writing my book and sell a million copies.
- I will show compassion to those around me.

This only takes a few minutes to do every morning. Please take some time to create your own affirmations and start meditating. You'll be surprised how many things start changing for you. Meditation will help jump-start your mind-set before the day even begins. Remember, the more you say them, the more you start to believe them, and then subconsciously, day by day, you will start to move from belief to action.

> *Prayer and Meditation works if you work it.*
> *Believe it or not, the choice is yours.*
> *~David G. Millen (second half of quote)*

~Notes~

36

_____
_____
_____
_____
_____
_____
_____
_____
_____
_____
_____
_____
_____
_____
_____
_____
_____
_____
_____
_____
_____
_____
_____
_____
_____

I'm Not Lucky Enough

37

Some of us hit the parent lottery when we were born, and there are countless others who hit parent purgatory. If life were a race, I would say the way in which we are raised will always be the core foundation of how we get out of the blocks. Some of us get out of the blocks fast and strong, while others come out stumbling, confused, and unsure of ourselves.

What is the parent lottery? In my opinion, you can be born into a rich family and still become a bum with no work ethic, spoiled, and lazy with a strong sense of entitlement. So, I'm not necessarily talking about parents who are financially stable and responsible (although that is a bonus). I'm talking about those parents who have a sound value base. That's when you're born into a family who works on teaching you values and morals. That's when you're born into a family who accepts and loves you for who you are. That's when you're born into a family who protects you from predators who are out to harm you. That's when you're born into a family who supports your dreams. That's when you're born into a family where the parents aren't perfect but their good role models. Again, they're not perfect, but they teach you more good lessons than bad ones. That's when you're born into a family who is willing to teach you valuable life lessons along your journey. That's when you're born into a family who teaches you how to work hard for everything you have, regardless if the parents are financially stable. Lastly, this is when you're born into a family who believes and values appropriate discipline and lessons when the children exhibit bad behavior or bad choices. In my opinion, parents are supposed to be the caregivers, protectors, and disciplinarians. They don't try to become the child's friend until that child is a grown adult.

If you did not have that luck of the draw, you had to or you have to fight and claw to learn certain lessons later on in life, as opposed to those who learned valuable lessons and had positive experiences early on in life. The moral of the story is this: whatever situation we were born into, we have to take away the excuse of luck. Don't get me wrong; we should always be grateful for the blessings that we started with, but we can't rest on those blessings to lift us to the next level of our lives. We also can't make excuses for why we don't have what we don't have.

When I was in college, we had a sign in our locker room. The sign read, "Luck is when preparation meets opportunity." The sign was placed right above the only door we walked out of before we hit the field for a home game. The head coach wanted us to see it and tap it right before we left the locker room every home game. I will never forget that sign. I tapped it for four years in a row, and it will forever resonate with me.

Have you ever heard people say comments like the following?

I am so lucky to have met my wife or husband. The reality is you prepared your mind-set over the years to be able to have those great and effective conversations with that other person. You prepared yourself over the years to share some of the same interests as the other person. You prepared yourself to grow into the person you are now. You were blessed to experience what you needed to experience to appreciate who you are, so you can be the best you for that other person. You also prepared your mind-set over the years to be able to compromise when need be and work as a team with this other person. You were not lucky to meet this person; you were prepared.

I am so lucky to have this job. The reality is, you prepared your skill set to a point that has propelled you to the position you have at your job or career.

That was a lucky catch, hit, or shot. The reality is, that person prepared for hours and hours in the weight room, in the film room, after practice, or during the off-season for that particular moment in the game.

You're lucky to live in that house. The reality is, this person had to prepare through savings and studying the market. This person had to prepare for the opportunity to get that job or start that career in order to make the money he or she makes to purchase the home or homes that he or she owns.

She's lucky to have a scholarship. The reality is, she prepared her mind and body for years to earn that scholarship. She sacrificed hours and hours of her time to make that scholarship a reality.

We must create our own luck through loads and loads of preparation. We never know when an opportunity is going to come our way. At any moment of the game or day, an opportunity may present itself. If we are prepared, the opportunity will be a great experience for us. If we're not prepared, the opportunity will pass us by and hurt like hell in the process. I simply say, we must look for opportunities that are around us and continue to prepare ourselves for when they arrive on our doorsteps.

*It's better to be prepared with no opportunity, than to
have an opportunity and not be prepared.*

~ Les Brown

~Notes~

37

I'm Not a Leader

38

Leader (noun): the person who leads or commands a group, organization, or country. The first to serve; the person who transforms his or her own thoughts and actions before asking or demanding that others transform their own.

I don't care if you're on your eighth grade basketball team, high school baseball team, college soccer team, just got promoted to management, or just started your own business. You have to lead. You were meant to lead! You must start by leading yourself, leading your mind, and leading by example. If you don't lead your troop now, your team will never have any true direction, and you will never be the leader or team that you are capable of being. If you lead with purpose and create and allow for moments of transition and transformation, you will positively start to change the culture of your environment.

The definition of a leader is not easy to pinpoint. There are so many layers and layers to work through and experience before one can truly become an effective leader. Being a leader is a constant work in progress. My goal for myself is to transform and learn something new about myself each and every day. I continuously want to put pieces of the puzzle together for myself as needed, so I can learn from my triumphs and from my failures.

Are Leaders Born or Made?

I believe great leaders are made, but it's still up to us to realize that we can lead when the opportunity presents itself. It's up to us to listen to sound advice from parents, mentors, coaches, teachers, and managers. It's up to us to study other leaders in person and through books and videos. It's up to us to learn from our mistakes and our unique experiences, good or bad. It's up to us to realize that we have something special inside of us that no one else in the world has. I definitely believe, that we're all born with unique talents and personalities. We all have great potential, and there will always be unique opportunities to lead in some capacity in our lives.

Here are a few questions I believe we all need to think about when it comes down to leadership: Will we take the time to develop our unique talents and potential, or will we let them lie dormant? Will we be smart enough to study, listen, and train to get better? And will we be bold enough and mature enough to lead when we must, even when we least expect to?

Leadership Advice

The following are a few points of reference that I continue to work through, study, and have actually used and experienced for myself. They help me navigate through the daily storm of leading myself and other human beings. I do great with some of these tips, and I need to continue to work on others. Fortunately, I now have these tools in my toolbox that I can refer back to and learn from on a daily basis. Hopefully, they can help you in your journey to lead yourself and others as well.

Surround Yourself with Great People

I don't care if you're twelve or seventy years old. The people you choose to surround yourself with the most are the people who are going to influence you the most. They are either influencing you positively or negatively. Okay, stop for a second right now and think about the people you surround yourself with daily. Who are they? Why do you choose to be in their presence consistently? Do they add to your life, or do they subtract from it? Do they bring positive energy, positive ideas, and positive support to your life, or do they bring negative energy, doubt, drama, and confusion? You are the only person who can honestly answer these questions for yourself. One of my mentors told me one day, "If you're the smartest person in your immediate group, then you're in the wrong group." We need people in our immediate circle whom we can learn from and feed off of. We need people who inspire us and push us to get better and be better on a consistent basis.

Find a Mentor

I try my best to speak with my mentors at least once a week. See, before I had a real live mentor, I would find countless mentors over the years in books, videos, and documentaries because real flesh-and-blood mentors did not come easy for me. In the past, when I had questions about how life works, I just simply turned to myself and my variety of self-help books and videos. I learned from some great mentors from afar, but there's still nothing like a real human connection to someone you admire and trust. Nothing can replace talking, listening, and having those face-to-face or phone conversations with successful people who have done or who are doing what you do or want to do. Talking with real people who already have the blueprint that you're looking for is priceless.

When you have those conversations, you get a chance to study the reflection of the person's voice. You get honest answers to your questions. You get a chance to hear stories that help you connect the dots, rather it be personal or professional. A good mentor will always inspire you and push you to do more. A good mentor will help you think differently than you ever have. A good mentor will make deposits into your life that will stay in your account for a life- time.

What Do Mentors Look Like?

- Mom
- Dad
- Siblings
- Pastor
- Business owner
- Friend

- Personal trainer
- Wellness or life coach
- Manager
- Boss
- Author
- Construction worker
- Real estate agent
- Financial planner
- High school, college, or professional Athlete
- Doctor
- Nurse
- Professor
- Teacher
- Actor
- Writer
- Maid
- Sanitation worker
- Millionaire
- Olympian

I hope you get the point. Take your time and find someone you trust and respect. Try your best to set up a time each week, biweekly, monthly, or every other month to check in and speak with the person directly. A great way to do this without physically being present is to use some type of video chatting tool like Sire, Google Hangout, or FaceTime. If the person is across town or out of state, you'll be able to video conference and still get the same effect as talking to him or her in person. Where there's a will, there's always a way.

Be Knowledgeable

Study, study, study your craft! There are people in our own neighborhoods who only have a formal high school education, but yet make over $100,000 a year. Why? Because they have trained, studied, and failed at their particular craft to the point, where they've learned how to master their special and unique skill set. Their skill set serves others in the our communities who are willing to pay them handsomely for their service.

See, we have to keep studying and learning about our craft on a daily basis. Whatever areas we feel we're weak in, we should study that. Whatever is new in our industry, we should study that. Take ten to fifteen minutes to read that article or that chapter. Listen to that audio book or motivational speaker on the way to work or school. Pay attention and take good notes at that conference or professional development course. Even if it's only one quote, one idea, or one brief story, we have to grab something that we can put into our knowledge toolbox and use at a later date. The more we know about different points of view, the more we'll be able to play devil's advocate in our own minds to defend or empathize with other people's point of view.

I always ask my students and athletes the following simple question when they are confused and refusing to get the information they need. The question is: Why did the squeaky wheel get oiled? Most of the time, they looked puzzled when I ask this question. The answer is very simple: Because it was squeaking! We have to squeak if we want the information we need. In the Bible, Matthew 7:7 reads, "Ask and it will be given to you; seek and you will find; knock and the doors will be open." If we ask loud and often enough, we will get what we need, when we need it. If we seek long enough, we will get what we need, when we need it, and if we knock hard enough, someone will eventually open the door.

The more we know, the more we can help others when they ask questions. Having and retaining information gives us huge amounts of credibility among our peers and those we are trying to lead. Also, don't be afraid to say you don't know something when asked. Please let people know that you will get the answer to their question as soon as possible or call someone on the spot and get the answer right then and there. We also must use these experiences to remind ourselves to continue to research and learn as much as we can about our given craft and about certain team members roles and responsibilities.

Once we get the information, we must try our best to retain it and put it to practice. We will always learn valuable lesson through failure and success when we practice. Are we talking about practice? Yes, practice! We learn the most during practice. We then apply what we learned at practice into the game and learn even more about ourselves and what we're made of during those games.

Have a Clear Goal or Vision

What I've learned in recent years is that people need to hear or see the team's goal or vision as often as possible. If the goal or vision is clear and stamped into people's minds, it's a lot easier for them to buy into the team or organization's vision. As a principal, I try my best to share our goals and vision whenever possible through staff meetings, motivational videos, team building activities, flyers, emails, intercom announcements, and a variety of inspirational quotes.

The Hardwood

I used to be my former school's seventh and eighth grade girls' basketball coach. I already know your question. How did I have time to do that and run a school? I found the time because sports and coaches helped save my life. If it were not for sports and the many coaches who sowed into my life, I don't know where I would be today. So, I took it upon myself to give back what was given to me. Anyway, I was the coach at my previous school for five years, and I'm proud to say that we won five straight championships, and in 2019, we had a perfect record of 20–0. And if you expand back to the previous season, that gave us a record of 30–0. Most of our success was due to our girls buying into our goals, our vision and our mission.

Our Team Goals

- **Push through the pain every day.**
  If we push through the pain, greatness is waiting on the other side.
- **Be your sister's keeper.**
  We have to look out for one another. If we don't, who will?
- **Play hard until the whistle blows.**

We have to give everything we have until the clock strikes 00:00. If we don't, we let ourselves and our teammates down. It will be hard to look at ourselves in the mirror because we know we didn't leave it all on the court.

- **Win every play.**
  Small victories add up throughout the game. Greatness is in the details!
- **Learn every day.**
  The more we learn; the better we get.
- **Play relentless defense** (and a championship will be on the way). Constant pressure versus obstacles will eventually knock them down.

Our Mission

- Play as one.
- Be accountable for your actions and your work on and off the court.
- Do what's hard today, so tomorrow will be easy.
- Make our presence known early and often.
- Break our opponents' will to win.
- "Winning isn't everything but trying our best to win is." (Vince Lombardi)

If you think coaching an eighth grade girls basketball team is easy, you're sadly mistaken. Not only do you have to coach the kids, you also have to coach the parents. You must get parent buy-in first before you can successfully move forward with your season. Some parents love to coach from the stands, so you have to set ground rules with your team and parents before the season starts. Parents have to understand that their babies are instructed to only listen to the coaches during games.

If they don't listen to me, they will be on the bench listening to their parents all game long. You have to remind parents to let you have their babies for two hours a day, and you promise to give them back.

I also had to deal with whining and crying from certain players when things were not going their way. Sometimes the whining and crying started with a few of my starters who thought they were special. I had to shut that down quickly and remind them, *"You are no good to us if your mind is not here. You're no good to us if you think you deserve special treatment. I will bench you for a quarter, a half, or an entire game if you can't get it together. If I kick you out of my practice, you will not be playing this week at all!"*

When players did things that hurt the team, they quickly find themselves on the bench. That usually straightens the bad attitudes up very quickly, along with some nice sprint work. 17s (sprinting from sideline to sideline 17 times, within a specific time frame over and over and over) will do the trick.

I really had to pay attention to detail when I was working with my teams. I had players who had experience and talent, and I also had players with no experience and limited talent. That forced me to stand firm on teaching and reteaching the fundamentals of the game.

When I gave hard criticism, I always built them back up before the end of practice. See, I had some players who thought they know it all, so I had to quickly break them down and show them their mistakes and bad habits. I break them down, and then I slowly build them back up. I always remind them that if they just listen and pay attention to the little things, their potential for greatness will be unlimited. I share these team strategies with you because they help me when I'm coaching my staff in certain areas as well.

Vision

Everyone will not be able to see your vision at first, but if you stay the course and keep working toward the vision as a collective organization, things will turn around. You definitely need team leaders or captains whom your team respects and trusts. Use them as much as possible to motivate the troops and guide them toward the vision. Sometimes they love hearing from them more than they like hearing from you. When the message comes from their peers (other experts in the field), the message penetrates a little deeper and starts to become part of their consciousness.

Coaches on the Floor

As a basketball coach, I tell my team captains: You must be coaches on the floor. You must coach your teammates as you play the game. I can only do so much from the sideline. You must take control and control the offense and defense from inside the ropes.

If we allow our department heads, managers, team leaders, or team captains to lead from the middle, the vision of our organization and the team cohesiveness will be pursued and developed at a much faster pace. Team members who are having a hard time buying into the process will slowly start to convert. We just have to meet with our team leaders consistently and trust the process. We also must remember that our team leaders need guidance and praise whenever time allows. They are the glue that will keep your team together and thriving. We also must make sure that our leadership meetings are productive because we can never get that time back. Meetings can be anywhere from ten minutes to an hour; it just depends on the day, the mission, and the situation. Lastly, we must remind our team leaders to remind the team that the door is always open to listen to their concerns or ideas.

Take Responsibility for Your Mistakes

Those who look to you for leadership and guidance need to feel that you are human. They need to feel that you don't think you are above reproach. When we start taking responsibility for our mistakes, it gives our teams the opportunity to view us as honest and trustworthy human beings. They need to know that we are willing to humble ourselves for the success of the individual, the group, or the entire organization.

I have legitimate excuses of why I can't visit as many classrooms as I should as an instructional leader. I have district meetings; parent meetings; preparing for school audits; creating and planning staff meetings; restorative justice circles; bullying, drugs, theft, weapons investigations; suspensions; budget concerns; master scheduling; and the list goes on and on. Do I use them? No. I just own it. I let my staff know that I have to get better and get more organized, so I can get to more classrooms—period.

I used to fall asleep in district staff meetings. Yes, fall asleep. District staff meetings are where all of the principals, assistant principals, and districts heads come together to discuss important information or participate in a training. Even when I was a teacher, I would fall asleep in staff meetings. No one wants to hear that I get up at three or four o'clock in the morning to work on my book, meditate, pray, read, or hit the gym. They don't want to hear about me being in the hospital late nights and early mornings with my wife who has lupus and legions on her brain or the fact that I must support my wife with taking care of my mother-in-law who has early stages of dementia and chronic seizures.

I simply need to lead by example, engage, and be professional wherever I am. I'm happy to say that I have stopped this practice. I had a good heart-to-heart conversation with a personal mentor, and I really started studying some of Dr. Eric Thomas's key speeches on leading by example. "Sleep is the new broke!" His motivational messages are the reason I get up so early, but I also had to start realizing that I must stay alert and focused throughout my entire day as well—no matter how tired I am. Also, the book *Mindset* by Dr. Carol S. Dweck helped change my mind-set and actions as well.

Praise in Public and Reprimand in Private

Praise: To express warm approval or admiration.
Reprimand: To criticize, correct, scold, rebuke.

I learned these two skills alone over many years of coaching experience.

- ❖ College football: one year as quarterback and wide receiver coach
- ❖ High school football: four years as offensive coordinator, quarterback, and wide receiver coach
- ❖ Pop Warner football: one year as head coach (one championship)
- ❖ High school basketball: two years as head coach (one championship)
- ❖ Middle school basketball: fourteen years as head coach (ten championships)
- ❖ Middle school baseball: four years as head coach (two championships)
- ❖ Track and field: four years

- ❖ Personal trainer: ten years (speed and agility and quarterback training)
- ❖ Personal trainer: (before college) DeShawn Shead – Defensive Back Seattle Seahawks and Detroit Lions
- ❖ Personal trainer: (before college) Josh Shaw – Defensive Back Cincinnati Bengals, Kansas City Chiefs, Tampa Bay Buccaneers, and Arizona Cardinals
- ❖ Assistant principal: four years
- ❖ Principal: two years

As coaches and leaders of men, women, and children, we must study and learn the personalities of those we are leading. When we pay close attention to our players and how they handle stress, success, and constructive criticism, it gives us the feedback we need for how we should individually communicate with the different personalities we work with on a daily basis. Through experience, we learn when we need to walk on eggshells and when we need to be more direct.

I consistently remind my teams and my captains that there is no one position on our team that is more important than the other. From the guard to the center, from the quarterback to the kicker, from the principal to the noon duty, all positions are valuable and important for our team to function at a high level. The only thing that differentiates us is our responsibilities and our pay grade. I believe the human value of each team member is always priceless.

When we praise people in the mist of their peers, it gives them a sense of pride and an added sense of worth to the team. We can all use a little praise every now and then. Sometimes a little praise will lift a person up and take him or her to the next level in their performance. As human beings, it's natural for us to want to feel valued and appreciated.

Reprimand

When we reprimand a team member in private opposed to in the public eye, it saves that person a lot of embarrassment and humiliation. When we do this, we also start to create an environment of trust and accountability.

Correction should be more of a teaching moment, if it absolutely has to be done amongst one's peers. When we must reprimand a team member, we should always do it with compassion and empathy. We also must work to communicate effectively, so we can help our team members change the behavior that is not warranted.

From my experience, it's always best to learn the personalities of those you are leading. We have to coach the same concepts but yet guide them in different ways. Let their personalities guide you during your reprimands and corrections.

Now, in my imperfect world, I do miss the mark on occasion when it comes to reprimanding students. Sometimes my emotions get the best of me, and I have to reprimand a student right on the spot because he or she is out of control and being disrespectful to staff members. Hey, I'm a work process. Pray for me.

Make People Feel Important

Tony Robbins is one of the most influential authors, motivational speakers, and life coaches of our generation. His research, along with other brilliant minds on his team, have come to the conclusion (through research) that there are six core human needs.

1. **Certainty:** the need for safety, stability, security, comfort, predictability, and consistency.
2. **Variety:** the need for variety, surprise, challenges, excitement, difference, chaos, and adventure.
3. **Significance:** the need to have meaning, feel special, feel wanted, sense of importance, and worth of love.
4. **Love and connection:** the need for communication, unified approval, and attachment to feel connected with, intimate, and loved by other human beings.
5. **Growth:** the need for constant emotional, intellectual, and spiritual development.
6. **Contribution:** the need to give beyond ourselves, to care, protect, and serve others.

Let's briefly focus on the need to feel significant. *The need to have meaning and special pride, to feel needed and wanted, and to have a sense of importance and worth of love.* If this is a core human need and we have an opportunity to supply it to people, why not do it? It does not cost much. It only costs a few moments of our time. It's a simple act of kindness that goes a long way for our team members, which eventually spreads to our entire organization.

When addressing team members, we need to make sure we say what we mean and mean what we say. People need to feel that we are sincere and that we care. Here a few examples.

- ❖ Great job!
- ❖ Nice work!
- ❖ I don't know how we made it without you.
- ❖ We couldn't have made it without you.
- ❖ You're doing a great job with your team.
- ❖ I wish we could duplicate you.
- ❖ You make my job so much easier.
- ❖ You're doing amazing work.
- ❖ Thank you for all of the time you put in.
- ❖ Your family comes first. Go home.
- ❖ Thank you for taking time away from your family to finish this campaign.
- ❖ Your commitment is incredible.
- ❖ Excellent idea! Let's do it.
- ❖ You're a great leader. Keep it up.

See how simple this is?

Be Persuasive

Being persuasive starts with passion and confidence. When we show passion for what we're talking about and what we're doing, people tend to pay more attention to what we're saying and doing. They can't help but notice how enthusiastic and excited we are about the subject matter. That passion will help start that slight paradigm shift in their minds, and that's all you need. Of course, if we have no passion or confidence in what we're saying and doing, our idea, argument, suggestion, or message will be shot down and fall on deaf ears from the start.

When we have evidence to back up our passionate idea, argument, or suggestion, that makes our message highly undeniable. If we have facts to show how great our idea is or how important the vision or goals are, it makes it hard for people to argue against our point of view and it forces them to follow proper protocol.

Emotions

Appeal to their emotions. In my experience, one of the best ways to appeal to peoples' emotions is by telling a story related to your topic. It could be a personal story or even a fictional story about someone else. You can use visual media, pictures, and music to assist with this as well. People love to create visual images in their minds, which help them connect to what you're saying. Most people love a good story. We love to imagine. We love adventure. We love to laugh. We love drama and triumph. We love mental breaks throughout the course of our day whenever we can get them.

To Die For (Story Time)

There were two golfers teeing off on the first hole at this beautiful golf course in Hawaii. This golf course had lakes, cliff shots, island shots, mountains, and, of course, great weather. The first fairway was very narrow and lined with palm trees on both sides. The first golfer to tee off was a former college golfer. He put his ball down on the tee, visualized his shot, took a few practice swings, and *bam*! The ball came off of his club like a jet taking off from a runway. His ball traveled 335 yards straight down that beautiful fairway.

The other golfer was not that good. He was big and athletic, but he probably played a round of golf once every six months. So, he teed his ball up, visualized his shot, took a few practice swings, and *bam*! The ball sounded like a shotgun coming off his club. To both of their surprise, he hit his ball straight down the middle of the fairway 315 yards. He couldn't believe it, and neither could his buddy.

As he walked up to his ball for his second shot, he noticed that his ball was sitting on top of an anthill. There were probably about four thousand ants on this hill, but his ball was teed up perfectly on top of this little hill. He's thinking, *Sweet!* So once again, he pulled out his club, visualized his shot, swung, and *bam!* He killed two thousand ants, missing the ball completely. He regrouped and tried it again. He visualized his shot, took a practice swing, and *bam!* He killed 1,995 more ants, completely missing the ball again. At this point, one of the ants looked at the other four ants that were left and said, "If we're going to survive this thing, we better get on the ball!"

The moral of the story? We have to lead, get on the ball, and make life-saving, team-saving, culture-saving, people-saving, and organizational-saving decisions. We definitely don't want to die with other companies, teams, relationships, dreams, and ideas that got smashed and are now in the graveyard.

People and Ideals We Trust the Most: Tell Great Stories

Think about it. The people we trust and/or listen to the most are people who share great stories. They have the ability to hold our attention for great lengths of time, whether it be for thirty seconds or an hour or two.

- Pastors
- Motivational speakers
- Politicians (Well, you may not trust many, but he or she told enough good stories for you to actually vote for him or her.)
- Singers
- Rappers
- Poets
- Professors
- Teachers
- Coaches
- Comedians
- Sitcoms
- Movies
- Mentors

Everyone or everything on this list you may not have trusted or believed in at first. But the more you heard the message and the better they became at storytelling, the easier it became for them to start gaining your trust and changing your mind-set.

Actions Speak Louder Than Words

"Do as I say, not as I do!" This approach does not work that often. It may work with small kids, but as they get older, they start to see through the foggy glass. It's hard for others to build trust and respect us if we seldom do not do what we are asking them to do. Leading by example is the foundation for others to follow our lead. It's simple and consistent.

Our kids, team members, employees, fans, and haters are always watching us. What we do will always be remembered way more than what we can ever say. I shared with you earlier that I would oftentimes fall asleep in staff meetings when I was a teacher and in district meetings. Unfortunately, that's all I will be remembered for in some people's minds, and that's no one's fault but mine. I own it, and I must continue to move forward and create a better legacy for myself with better actions.

Integrity

Integrity is something we all need to work on and work out on a daily basis. None of us are perfect, so we must continue to work on being the best versions of ourselves daily. What we do behind closed doors when no one is watching, is the best indicator of where our integrity compass is pointing in that moment in time. It also goes back to doing what we said we were going to do with no excuses.

Again, none of us are perfect, but the goal should be to consistently work on ourselves and feel good about the daily choices we make. When we make mistakes, we should try our best to learn from them and move forward. Our moral compass will always be tested and moving, as we navigate through various stages of our lives. When we do miss the mark, the good thing is that as long as we're breathing, we will always be given other opportunities to do better. Hopefully, as we mature and learn different lessons, we will start making better decisions that work for us and for those we are trying to lead and protect.

You Can't Please Everyone

If you know too much, some people will think you're arrogant. If you don't have answers right away, some people will think you know nothing. If you have a strong and confident personality, some people will think you're arrogant and unapproachable. If you need to improve in certain areas, some people will think you will never get stronger and better. If you're a serious person by nature, some people will think you need to lighten up. If you have a good sense of humor, some people will think you're too silly and not serious enough. If you're consistently nice to people, some people will try to take your kindness for weakness. If you dress too nice, some people will think you're conceded. If you dress too casually, some people will think you're a slob and unprofessional.

People will always have an opinion about you. We can't control what people think. We can only control what we think and what we do and say on a daily basis. We can't drive ourselves crazy trying to please everyone. It's not possible. When we find ourselves trying to do that, we only stress ourselves out and we're the only ones who lose.

We have to please ourselves by consistently working on ourselves and our crafts. Don't get me wrong; I believe we should constantly be evolving to make ourselves better people but not for the sake of pleasing others. We have to stay true to who we are. Once we lose the core of who we are, we lose ourselves.

I love this quote: "You can't please all of the people all of the time; and it's very hard to please some of the people some of the time; so you might as well try to please yourself all of the time and stay true to yourself and your purpose."

Are you just a boss, instead of a leader? Do you wield power, instead of transforming yourself, your workers, your team, or your organization? Being a good leader is a process. Lead with purpose and a growth mindset and they will follow.

~ Dr. Carol S. Dweck

~Notes~

38

The Odds Are Too Great, Part II

(A Football Life)

39

The position of quarterback is a small fraternity of leaders who have to lead their teams and set the highest example of mental strength on and off the field. Unfortunately, the black athlete has been stereotyped for decades when it comes to playing the position of quarterback. Many talented black quarterbacks in the sixties, seventies, eighties, and nineties chose to switch their position or were volun-told to switch their position to wide receiver or defensive back once they moved into the NFL.

For those who may not know or for those who may have forgotten: In America's history, the black athlete was rarely given a chance to excel at the position of quarterback until brave coaches and brave players broke through the glass ceiling of prejudice and discrimination. The stereotype that the black athlete did not have the mental capacity to handle the pressures that the quarterback position encompassed has not only been proven wrong but has been shattered throughout America's football history. Once these incredible men were given a chance to excel, the sky was the limit. Of course, it did not come without the cost of struggle, darkness, judgement, doubters, insults, death threats, pain, uncertainty, and self-doubt.

In the past twenty years or so, we have consistently started seeing a variety of different quarterbacks of color all across the nation, leading high school, college, and professional teams to great heights. It's great to see the evolution of the quarterback position and how teams are now putting the best and smartest quarterback/athlete available (rather he be black, white, blue, or green) at that position to lead and learn while doing so.

Being a quarterback since the age of twelve, I have to mention my top ten NFL quarterbacks (out of many) who have inspired and paved the way for me and countless others. I've had a chance to meet and watch some of these men play in my lifetime, and others I've had to research their courage, redemptions, and greatness. The odds were never too great for these men. They made it possible for little boys, especially little boys who look like me, to dream big. Throughout these men's lives on and off the field, they had to throw away all excuses and rise to the occasion of greatness. Some had to rise even higher to excel when they were confronted and challenged with their own personal mistakes and demons. They were forced to stand firm on the values they believed in with the world watching and judging.

Doug Williams

He was the first African American quarterback to win a Super Bowl in the NFL. He led the Washington Redskins to victory in Super Bowl XXII against the Denver Broncos in 1986. He was the first player in Super Bowl history to throw four touchdowns in a half and the only quarterback to throw four touchdowns in a single quarter. He was also named Super Bowl MVP.

He attended Grambling State University (HBCU-Historically Black Colleges and Universities) from 1974–1977 before he was drafted in the first round in 1978 by the Tampa Bay Buccaneers. In college, he was 46–7 as a starting quarterback, winning three Southwestern Athletic Conference Championships in the process. He was also forth in Heisman Trophy votes his senior year (1977), leading the NCAA in passing yards (3,286) and touchdown passes (38).

From the very beginning with the Tampa Bay Buccaneers, he led a two-win team (the previous season) to the 1979 NFC Championship Game. He was the only African American starting quarterback in the NFL during that time period, and he was the lowest paid starting quarterback during that time period as well. At the time, there were twelve backups in the league who made more money than he did that season.

Doug Williams was a pioneer who stood the test of time, from death threats to unequal pay. He fought on and off the field for what was right. Mr. Williams is an inspirational family man and successful businessman today. When you get a free moment, please treat yourself to his amazing story. The NFL Network did a great piece on him. Please watch *A Football Life: Doug Williams*.

Marlin "The Magician" Briscoe

He was a starting quarterback from the time he started playing Pop Warner football. He started all through high school and all through his college career at Omaha University. He was drafted by the Denver Broncos in 1968, not as a quarterback but as a defensive back. He got his shot to play quarterback on September 29, 1968, versus the Boston Patriots. During the game, the starting quarterback went down with an injury and the backup was not performing well at all. He was finally called upon to see if he could give his team some type of spark. He went on to throw for a rookie record (fourteen touchdowns) that season and runner-up for Rookie of the Year.

The next game, he was named the starter. He became the first black starting quarterback in the American Football League. He played one year with the Denver Broncos before he was traded to the Buffalo Bills, where he became an All Pro at wide receiver. He led his team in receptions and touchdowns the three seasons he was there. After his third season with the Bills, he was traded to the Miami Dolphins. He became an All Pro wide receiver with the Dolphins and won two Super Bowls (VII and VIII) in the process. He was part of the 1972 Dolphin team that went undefeated and is the only team in NFL history that has accomplished that feat. He played nine years in the NFL before he retired with the New England Patriots. He faced some hard demons and setbacks with drug addiction during his NFL journey but fought back to take control of his life. He was a great athlete and is still a great ambassador for the game. Please watch *The Magician: The Story of Marlin Briscoe*.

Warren Moon

Warren Moon played college football for the University of Washington. He led the Huskies to a Rose Bowl win over Michigan his senior year in 1977. Moon did not get selected in the 1978 NFL draft, so he took his talents to the CFL (Canadian Football League). In six seasons with the Edmonton Eskimos, he threw for 2, 228 yards and led the Eskimos to five straight Grey Cup Championship wins from 1978–1982. He's also a two-time Grey Cup MVP. He was inducted into the Canadian Football Hall of Fame in 2001.

He started his seventeen-year career in the NFL in 1984 with the Houston Oilers. He was named the NFLs Walter Payton Man of the Year in 1989. In 1990, he was the NFLs passing leader and Offensive Player of the Year. He was also selected to the Pro Bowl nine times in his career. In his long journey in the NFL, he threw for 49,325 yards. He was also inducted into the Pro Football Hall of Fame in 2006. He is also the first African American quarterback in the history of the NFL that was inducted into the Pro Football Hall of Fame. Please watch *A Football Life: Warren Moon*.

In his career bio, he states, "I started wearing number one in college because I always wanted to be the No. 1 guy. I always want to remind my teammates, that I'm the man who can get it done."

James "Shack" Harris

He played college football for the Grambling State Tigers (HBCU) from 1965–1968. He led his team to four straight Southwestern Athletic Conference (SWAC) titles during his outstanding college career. He was also named MVP of the 1967 Orange Blossom Classic. He played in the NFL from 1969–1981. He was the first black quarterback to start an entire season for the Buffalo Bills. During his long career, he played for the Buffalo Bills, Los Angeles Rams, and the San Diego Chargers. He was selected to the Pro Bowl and also won the Pro Bowl MVP in 1974. He was definitely a trailblazer who led the way for many black quarterbacks to follow. I feel very fortunate that I was able to meet him back in 2008 when he was a scout for the Jacksonville Jaguars. Please look up and watch *The Legend of NFL Quarterback James "Shack" Harris.*

Steve "Air" McNair

Steve McNair is one the toughest quarterbacks I've ever seen play the game. No matter how many times he got hit and beat up during a game, he always got back up. He was an iron man on the field. He did whatever it took to help his team win football games. He attended college at Alcorn State University (HBCU) from 1991–1994. During his senior year, he threw for 5,337 yards and fifty-six touchdowns. He won the Walter Payton Award as the top Division I-AA player of the year and also finished third in the Heisman Trophy race that year. He was the third overall pick in the 1995 NFL Draft by the Houston Oilers. He led the Tennessee Titan's to Super Bowl XXXIV versus the Rams and lost by one yard, getting stopped at the one yard line with no seconds left on the clock. In his thirteen-year NFL career, he threw for 31,304 yards and 174 touchdowns. He was selected to the Pro Bowl three times and was co-MVP of the league in 2003. Please watch, *A Football Life: Steve McNair.* He had an awesome career but a tragic ending to his very short life at the early age of thirty-six.

Randall Cunningham

This man has got to be one of the most exciting quarterbacks to ever play in the NFL, along with Michael Vick and a rising star by the name of Lamar Jackson. What can I say? Randall Cunningham was Houdini in cleats. His escape-ability was incredible! Randall Cunningham attended college at UNLV and led his team to an 11–2 record his senior year in 1984. He was drafted by the Philadelphia Eagles in the second round of 1985. During his incredible career, he was selected to four Pro Bowls, earned league MVP (1998), player of the year (1990), comeback player of the year (1992), and was inducted into the Philadelphia Eagles Hall of Fame in 2009.

He played fifteen years in the NFL. The two most notable teams he played for are the Philadelphia Eagles (1985–1995) and the Minnesota Vikings (1997–1999). In 1998, he led the Vikings to a 15–1 record. I thought for sure this team was going to the Super Bowl that year. He had two weapons on both sides of the field all year long. Hall of Famers Randy Moss and Chris Carter simply destroyed the league that year. In the NFC Championship game, they came within a last-minute field goal from advancing to the Super Bowl game. In Cunningham's exciting career, he threw for 29,979 yards, 207 touchdowns, and 35 rushing touchdowns. If you have never seen him play, please go to YouTube right now and look at his highlight reel. It is simply amazing!

I'm proud to say that I got a chance to meet and chat with this man in Las Vegas in 1994 when I was playing in the CFL. We had a quick conversation one day after one of my practices. At the time, I was playing for a new CFL expansion team that is now defunct (the Las Vegas Posse). It was an amazing experience to actually meet one of my inspirations in person. If you want to go deeper into his amazing football life; please check out *A Football Life: Randall Cunningham*.

Michael Vick

Arguably, he is one of the most dynamic quarterbacks to ever play in the NFL. He ran 4.25 seconds in the forty-yard dash, which simply means, he was one of the fastest and most explosive athletes in the league. It is simply shocking to see any man run that fast, especially a quarterback. The football world had never seen a quarterback this explosive and this athletic since Randall Cunningham. But, unlike Cunningham, Michael Vick was pure lighting in a bottle. Like lighting, he struck quick, and he was always electrifying. He was a highlight reel in motion. Every time he touched the football, you had to sit on the edge of your seat because you never knew what he was going to do next. He had every person in the stadium and everyone watching at home on their heels, excited with anticipation. His legs were lethal weapons, and his arm was like a rocket launcher. Opposing defenses hated to face him because they knew in the blink of an eye, he could change the game. Defensive linemen knew they would have to chase him and chase him and chase him around that field all game long. The Michael Vick experience was in full effect.

After only playing two dynamic seasons for Virginia Tech and finishing third in the Heisman vote, he was selected number one overall in the 2001

NFL draft. He was drafted by the Atlanta Falcons. He played for the Atlanta Falcons from 2001–2006. In that time span, he earned three Pro Bowl appearances.

For those who don't know, at the height of his career, he got caught up in the famous Bad News Kennel scandal, involving dog fighting, gambling, and killing dogs. He was convicted and sentenced to two years in prison and lost his entire fortune that he worked so hard for during his career. He signed a massive contract with the Falcons for $130 million dollars, and in the blink of an eye, it was gone. Bad investments, creditors, legal fees, and fines led him to file for bankruptcy. I was highly disappointed, but I was hopeful that this man could and would redeem himself one day.

After serving his sentence, he signed with the Philadelphia Eagles. He served his time and came back to the league a changed man. He owned his mistakes, paid his debt to society, and was now ready to face the pressure, ridicule, judgement, and responsibility that was waiting for him from the public, the fans, the NFL, and his new teammates. He said in an interview, "Going to prison was the best thing that ever happened to me. If I don't go to prison, I would've never changed."

The Eagles and Coach Reed, were the only organization with a head coach willing to take a chance on him. They gave him that second chance. I believe we all deserve at least a second chance at some point in our lives.

In 2010, he had the greatest statistical season of his career and was named to his fourth Pro Bowl and was also named the NFLs Comeback Player of the Year. He threw for 3,018 yards and twenty-one touchdowns and rushed for nine. He also had 676 rushing yards that season. The Michael Vick experience was switched on one last time for all to witness and appreciate. The Eagles were so impressed with his play, his character, and his leadership skills, they decided to sign him to a six-year deal worth $100 million dollars.

In his thirteen-year career, he threw for 22,464 yards and 133 touchdowns. He also rushed for 6,109 yards, an NFL record for quarterbacks. He retired with the Pittsburgh Steelers in 2015 as a backup to Ben Roethlisberger. He reminds us all that redemption is a beautiful thing, we all should have a chance to experience. If you haven't already, please watch *A Football Life: Michael Vick*.

Russell Wilson

This man makes the quarterback position look so easy. He rarely makes mistakes that cost his team on game day. He's the constant professional on and off the field, always leading by example. At only 5'10 and 215 pounds, he has broken into the NFL like a gangbuster and made no way into his way. The prototypical height for an NFL quarterback is 6'4. He doesn't even come close to that. This man was drafted in the third round by the Seattle Seahawks in 2012—the third round.

He went into training camp his rookie year as the third quarterback on the depth chart. He fought and clawed his way to the top of that depth chart by outplaying his counterparts during the preseason. By the end of preseason, it was obvious who the starting quarterback was going to be when the regular season started.

His scrambling ability, leadership skills, pinpoint accuracy, preparation, and thinking ability is something special to watch every Sunday.

He was the lowest paid starting quarterback in the league his rookie season and never complained. He put on his hard hat and went to work every day for himself and his teammates. He is the face of the franchise and represents the Seahawks the way a professional leader is supposed to.

He was the 2012 NFL Rookie of the Year. In just his second season (2013), he led the Seahawks to their first Super Bowl championship. They completely dominated Peyton Manning and the Denver Broncos in Super Bowl XLVIII. Since 2012, he has been selected to six Pro Bowls. He's been a Pro Bowler every season he's been in the NFL, except for 2016.

With all of his accomplishments, he still never complained about being one of the lowest paid quarterbacks in the league his first three years. He was a man of his word, so he completed his three-year rookie contract. His loyalty and professionalism paid off in 2015. He signed a four-year contract extension worth $87.6 million with a $31 million signing bonus. Needless to say, he is no longer the lowest paid quarterback in the league. He is now one of the highest paid.

Here are few more of his statistics to date: He was the NFLs passing touchdown leader in 2017, and his level of play just continues to elevate each year. So far in his short career, he has thrown for more than 28,000 yards and more than 215 touchdowns, rushed for more than 3,900 yards, rushed for more than 20 touchdowns, completed 64 percent of his passes, and has a passer rating of 100.3. He has led his team to the playoffs every year he has been in the league, along with two Super Bowl appearances.

He was an undersized third-round pick. The odds were definitely against him. He made a way out of no way. He's an inspiration for his generation, especially the little boys and girls who are undersized at their positions. He gives hope that if you work hard and prepare yourself, anything is possible. You can find him now at your local grocery store on a Wheaties cereal box. He is the face of his franchise and a constant professional on and off the field. If you haven't already; please watch tons of highlights of him on YouTube. You will not be disappointed. I personally believe this man is a future Hall of Famer. His best is yet to come.

Joe Gilliam Jr.

During his junior and senior year at Tennessee State (HBCU), he was an All-American. He led his team to two championships with a 19–1 record. He was drafted in the eleventh round by the Pittsburgh Steelers in 1972. He actually outperformed Hall of Fame quarterback Terry Bradshaw in the preseason of 1974. He started six games before his lackluster performance got him benched. Once Terry Bradshaw got his starting position back, he never looked back and led the Steelers to four Super Bowls with Gilliam as his back up for the first two (Super Bowl IX and X). Former players have been quoted saying, "He was one of the most talented quarterbacks in the league, and he was better than Bradshaw." Bradshaw was even quoted saying, "I didn't beat him out. He gave me the position back." But Gilliam's battle with drug abuse affected his decision-making skills on and off the field, which ultimately cost him his starting job and his NFL career after only four short years.

For me, Gilliam represents talent and opportunity that was taken for granted. He was a pioneer with all of the physical tools, but he was never able to perfectly blend work ethic, talent, discipline, and leadership skills together. His life story is heartbreaking. It's a story of triumph and defeat of what could have been.

Joe Gilliam is an inspiration of what is possible and what can be taken away if you don't continue to work hard once given an opportunity. Please go to YouTube if you want to watch his highlights and hear what other NFL players (including Hall of Famers) had to say about this man, Mr. Joe Gilliam Jr.

Donavan McNabb

Donavan McNabb was a winner. He could stand in the pocket and deliver the ball with accuracy, or he could use his legs when he needed to make a play for his team. He was the second overall pick in the 1999 NFL draft. He was drafted out of Syracuse University where he passed for 8,389 yards and 77 touchdowns and was the Big East Offensive Player of the Year three out of the four years he played at Syracuse.

He was drafted by the Philadelphia Eagles and had great success. He led the Eagles to eight playoff appearances and one Super Bowl appearance. He led the Eagles to Super Bowl XXXIX, which they lost to New England 24–21. (Damn you, Tom Brady!) He played the game with heart and toughness. He never made excuses. Good or bad, he owned his play each week and came out the next week determined to play better than the last time he was on the field.

McNabb is the fourth quarterback in NFL history to amass more than 30,000 passing yards, 200 TD passes, 3,000 rushing yards and 20 rushing touchdowns in his career. He gave me hope that more and more quarterbacks (who looked like me) were headed to the NFL to stay. It was a pleasure to watch him play. He has great highlights on YouTube.

Honorable Mention

Colin Kaepernick

(Fellow alumni of the University of Nevada, Reno. I was the first African American quarterback to start and play at the University of Nevada [1989–1992], and he was the second [2006–2010].)

For those who don't know, Colin Kaepernick played professional football for the San Francisco 49ers from 2011–2016. In that short time span, he led the 49ers to Super Bowl XLVII against the Baltimore Ravens. He was one pass completion away from winning it all. Unfortunately, he came up one completion short on his last offensive play of the game. He was a duel threat using both of his legs and his arm to carve up defenses.

The main reason he is on my honorable mention list is because he sacrificed his pro football career to stand for something he believed in. He used his first amendment right to peacefully protest (kneeling on one knee during the singing of the National Anthem) against police brutality, on the biggest stage in the world—that stage being the national broadcast of NFL football games during the singing of the National Anthem.

He made it clear to everyone that he was not protesting the National Anthem or our armed forces. He was clearly protesting the senseless killings of young black men across the country by police officers. That took a lot of courage for him to put his job on the line to help the country and those in power start a dialogue and action plans regarding police brutality, especially concerning young black men. He sparked other players across the league to start protesting during the National Anthem as well.

He eventually got cut from his team for consistent "poor quarterback play." Supporters for Kaepernick would say, after he was cut, no other team in the league would give him a chance for employment because of the backlash the organization would get from fans and other organized groups. No matter how much he could help another team, the owners simply stayed away from this "bigger than life" controversial topic and figure.

The national debate that Kaepernick sparked divided football fans and nonfootball fans all across the county. Some thought he should've never used the NFL stage to protest during the National Anthem. They believe he and others disrespected the flag and the armed forces by exercising their first amendment rights. They believe he should've protested away from his job.

Others applaud his efforts for trying to bring more awareness to police brutality and senseless killings of young black men across the country. Nike even got on board airing one of their Just Do It campaigns. The commercial (with Kaepernick as the narrator) supports those who stand tall for what they believe in. The message being, *"Believe in something, even it means sacrificing everything!"* I will always have much respect for any man who takes a stance for a cause bigger than himself.

Lamar Jackson

Lamar Jackson, in my opinion, is one of the most dynamic athletes to play the quarterback position since Michael Vick. He's a mixture of Russell Wilson, Michael Vick, Steve Young, and Barry Sanders in one body. If you know anything about football, you understand that merging those four players together creates one bad man. That man would be Lamar Jackson.

While attending Louisville in college (2015–2017), he threw for 9,043 yards and 69 touchdowns. He rushed for 4,132 yards and 50 touchdowns. He accounted for 119 touchdowns in only three seasons as a collegiate quarterback. After his sophomore year in 2016, he became the youngest player in history (nineteen) to win the Heisman Trophy (the most prestigious award in college football).

College Awards

- Heisman Trophy (2016)
- Maxwell Award (2016)
- Walter Camp Award (2016)
- Associated Press Player of the Year (2016)
- Sporting News Player of the Year (2016)
- All-American (2016)
- ACC Player of the Year (2016, 2017)
- ACC Offensive Player of the Year (2016, 2017)
- ACC Athlete of the Year (2018)

Surprisingly, he was still the last quarterback selected in the 2018 NFL draft (round one, pick 32). Regardless of the big numbers and impressive wins he accounted for in college, he was still considered by top NFL analyst, scouts, coaches, and general managers, to be a project of a player that struggles throwing the ball and will never be able to sustain his running ability at the NFL level.

What I love about this young man is that he is very humble, and he continues to show mental toughness, amazing work ethic, and a high football IQ each and every week. He consistently proves his critics wrong on a weekly basis.

In his second year (2019) as a starting quarterback with the Baltimore Ravens, he shattered records that many thought he would never come close to. As I write this paragraph on December 7, 2019, at 9:03 a.m., he is the NFLs frontrunner to win the leagues' MVP.

As of December 8, 2019, he's "only" thrown for 2,677 passing yards and 28 touchdowns, and he's "only" rushed for 1,017 yards and 7 touchdowns (again) after only week thirteen of the 2019 NFL season. This isn't bad for a man many said would never make it as an NFL quarterback and was best suited to be a wide receiver.

Lamar Jackson: NFL Statistics as of Week Thirteen (2019)

- Touchdowns–Interceptions: 28–6
- Completion percentage: 64%
- Passer rating: 100.9

Lamar Jackson: NFL Records (As of December 8, 2019)

- Youngest player with five touchdown passes in multiple games
- First player to complete 75 percent of his throws with twelve-plus touchdown passes over a three-game span
- Most rushing yards by a quarterback in a three-game span: 338 (weeks 5–7 2019)
- Most perfect passer ratings in a season (2019)
- First quarterback to rush for 1,500-plus yards and pass for 3,000-plus yards in his first two seasons
- Youngest player (twenty-two) with multiple five-touchdown-pass games in NFL history
- Youngest player to be named Offensive Player of the Week four times in one season
- First quarterback with four multiple one-hundred-yard rushing games in a season (2019)

Most of these numbers will most definitely change for the simple fact that he is only in week thirteen of the 2019 season as I write this section of the book. It's amazing to me how he has accomplished all of this in such a short time frame.

Lamar Jackson is a phenomenal athlete who happens to play quarterback. He runs the ball and makes cuts like Barry Sanders. He runs a 4.3-second forty-yard dash and is able to cut on a dime, making defenders miss at will. His scrambling ability and decision-making skills match those of Russell Wilson and Steve Young. He is simply revolutionizing the game with his play. He is definitely must-watch television.

He lead his Baltimore Ravens team into the 2019 playoffs with a full head of steam. They entered the post season with the number one seed and a first round bye. Unfortunately, they fell hard in their first playoff game to the Tennessee Titans.

Although he did not make it to his ultimate destination, the Super Bowl, he was selected to the 2019 Pro Bowl Team and he was awarded the NFLs (2019) MVP.

Please do yourself a favor; if you haven't already and pull up some highlight clips of Mr. Lamar Jackson on YouTube. He has definitely silenced all critics with his elite quarterback play and leadership skills thus far. His best is yet to come. Hopefully next season he will light the NFL on fire once again and go for another post season push towards the Super Bowl.

The feeling of success is a special one and this feeling becomes magical when you achieve success against all odds in life!

~ Avijeet Das

~SECOND HALF~

Picture These Excuses

~

Born & Raised

STRAIGHT
OUT OF
COMPTON

Coach ~ Gatlin

Nothing Good Comes Out of the City of Compton

40

Compton is best known for the rap group NWA, the movie *Straight Outta Compton*, political misconduct, and the gang and drug violence that has occurred in my city over the past forty-plus years. Through it all, we still persevered as a community to the best of our ability and a lot of quality Comptonians (people from Compton) have done many great things for our community, the nation, and the world.

A Few Facts about Compton ~ "The Hub City"

The city of Compton is and for decades has always been considered the Hub City. People would move to Compton back in the thirties, forties, and fifties because it is centrally located in the county of Los Angeles and the city of Compton residents had and still have quick access to major freeways. You can literally get to work in cities like Long Beach, Carson, Marina del Rey, downtown Los Angeles, San Pedro, Pasadena, Watts, Palos Verdes, Beverly Hills, and Hollywood within fifteen minutes.

City of Compton: The Hub City

Compton used to be considered an inner suburb of Los Angeles from the thirties through the sixties. The city had a high percentage of white residents until the Watts riots in 1967. According to historian and director of the Center of Southern California Studies at California State University, Northridge Josh Sides, one of the main reasons for the influx of white residents in the early forties and fifties was due to racially restrictive covenants and deeds that prohibited African Americans and other races from living on a property. Middle-class African Americans slowly started moving into the thriving city after the US Supreme Court's ban on restrictive covenants in 1948.

(Owner of Image: Gatlin) Compton Court House

After the Watts riots in 1965, the white population began moving out, and African American and Hispanic populations started moving in. The term *white flight* was coined as the popular phrase in the sixties when white people started moving out of the inner city.

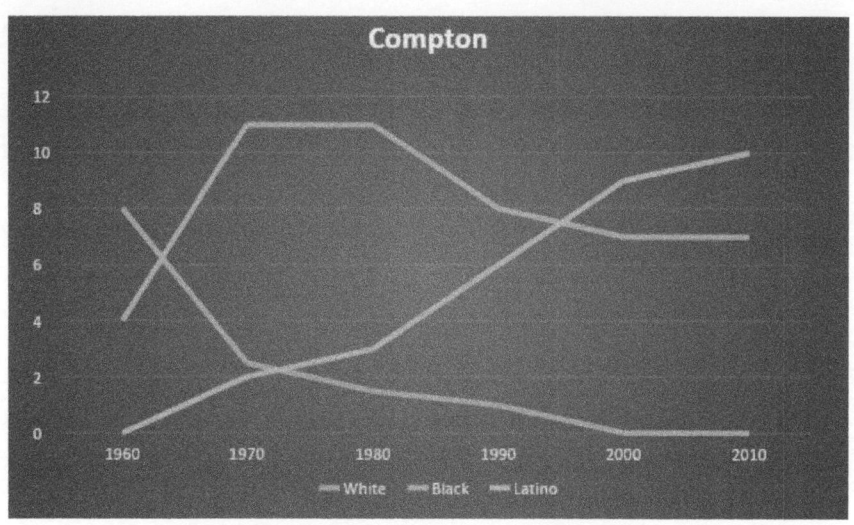

The Rise and Decline of Different Populations in Compton (The Compton Clash: Race Relations)

(Chart Recreated by: Gatlin, F.) [2=20%, 4=40%, 6=60%, 8=80%, 10=100%]

Street gangs such as the Crips and Bloods started their rise of productive organized crime and violence in 1969, along with the rise of unemployment and poverty throughout the city. When crack cocaine hit the scene in the eighties, the gangbanging environment and organized crime rose to another level of illegal money being made, senseless violence, and the erosion of human values. Gang violence continued to climb after the 1992 Rodney King riots, which caused a lot of middle-class black families (black flight) to move out and into other cities.

Notable Community Leaders Who Were Raised in Compton or Lived in Compton

Civic Leaders

❖ **Isadore Hall III** ~ Former member of the California State Assembly from the Sixty-fourth District. Fifty-second District (2008–2012).

- ❖ **Aja Brown** - Eighteenth Mayor of Compton, assumed office on July 2, 2013.
- ❖ **George H. W. Bush & Barbara Bush** - Former president of the United States (forty-third) and First Lady. Former residents of Compton in 1949 (Santa Fe Gardens).
- ❖ **Doris A. Davis** - First female mayor of a major metropolitan city (1973–1977).

Athletes

- ❖ **Venus and Serena Williams** - Two of the greatest tennis players to every play the game. They hold forty-six major titles and eight Olympic gold medals between the two.
- ❖ **Pete Rozelle** - Former NFL Commissioner (1960–1989).
- ❖ **Tyson Chandler** - NBA player and world champion with the Dallas Mavericks. 2012 Olympic gold medal team. Drafted out of Dominguez High School. (Professional Career 2001–present.)
- ❖ **Violet Palmer** - First female professional sports official in the United States, NBA and WNBA.
- ❖ **Richard Sherman** - NFL player and Super Bowl champion.
- ❖ **Ulis Williams** - Olympic gold medalist (track and field 4x400, Tokyo, 1964). Former Compton College president and superintendent (1996–2005).
- ❖ **Kimberly Anyadike** - Youngest African American woman (at fifteen) to pilot a plane solo across the United States.

Arts and& Entertainment

- ❖ **Kevin Costner** - Actor: *The Untouchables, The Bodyguard, Draft Day, Hidden Figures, Yellowstone*
- ❖ **Anthony Anderson** - Comedian and actor: *Blackish*
- ❖ **Kendrick Lamar** - Rapper, actor, producer, and activist
- ❖ **Niecy Nash** - Actress and comedian: *Claws*
- ❖ **Marilyn Monroe** - Actress and model
- ❖ **The Game** - Rapper, writer, and producer

- ❖ **Ice Cube ~ (South Central)** ~ Rapper, actor, producer, writer, director, and entrepreneur
- ❖ **Dr. Dre** ~ Rapper, producer, writer, actor, entrepreneur; Sold Beats by Dre for $3 billion dollars.

The Salvation Army saved a lot of lives. Right off of Santa Fe and Compton Boulevard.

Kept kids off of the streets during the summer months. (Owner of Image: Gatlin, F.)

(Owner of Image: Gatlin)

Chester and Myrrh

Chester block is where I grew up in the mist of Santana Block, around the corner from the Santa Fe Gardens Projects. I have a lot of great memories on this street. We had water balloon fights; football and basketball games; fireworks; and slush, donut, and ice cream trucks. Surprisingly, there were also two parents in almost every house on the block.

**Compton Community College (middle of)
Campus (Owner of Images: Gatlin, F.)**

Compton College Football Field (Owner of Image: Gatlin, F.)

This was and still is the foundation of our community. They held summer camps for the youth, festivals, youth track meets, football games, town hall meetings, community leader-guest speakers, debates, and spoken word venues. As a foster youth, this is where I went after school the second semester of my senior year to learn about independent living skills. This is also where I trained during the summer months in high school to get ready for the upcoming seasons. I can't count how many times I sprinted up those bleachers and ran hundreds.

The city of Compton is full of greatness and hidden gems. We just had to go out and use the resources that were presented us.

"Compton shaped and molded so many of us."
We Grew Like the Palm Trees of Compton

(Owner of Image: Gatlin, F.)

You Will Not Make It if You Have This Baby

41

To Be or Not to Be

"You will not make it, if you have this baby." That's what the doctor told my mom when she was pregnant with me at Dominguez Hills Hospital in Compton, California. Guess what, she had me anyway. Unfortunately, my mother went back home four years later, struggling to raise me and give me what she didn't have. Thank God she didn't buy into the excuse, "You will die if you have this baby." If it were not for my mom's courage to fight for what she believed in, there never would have been a Coach Gatlin. I would have never gotten a chance to go on so many journeys with so many different people. Thank you Mom, for giving me life.

Thank You ~ Shirley Maxie ~ My Mom

 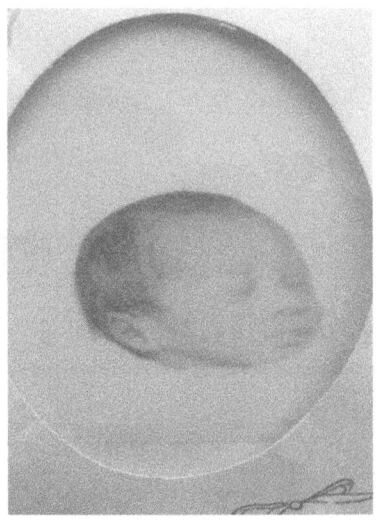

Mom (Owner of Image: Gatlin, F.)   **Coach Gatlin (Owner of Image: Gatlin, F.)**

Family Tree

(Owner of Image: Gatlin, F.)

Mom was incredible. She had to take care of all of my siblings before I was even born. The year is 1965. I was born six years later. From left to right in the back row: Ben, James, Ray, and Glenn. Front row: Marie and Arthur. Bo-Bo is the man in the picture. He is the father of Arthur. Mom gave me his last name, and I never looked back. He and my mom broke up before I was born.

Who's not pictured here are three important people I grew up with: Boom, Cat, and Kevin. These are my cousins I was raised with in Compton. I consider them my siblings after years of growing up in the same house and sharing cherished memories. They all inspired me (through the years) to play football and go to college.

I Can't Raise Any More Kids ~ It's Just Too Much

42

This is what I looked like when I was four years old. Thank goodness, Margie Rasco (my aunt) and T (the man who accepted me into his family) never accepted this excuse. The day my mom went back home, they took me and my sister to Compton, California, from San Pedro, California, and raised us like we were their own. This was the 2nd best decision anyone has ever made for me. Of course, the best decision ever made for me was when my mom decided not to let the doctor kill me.

Fantastic 4

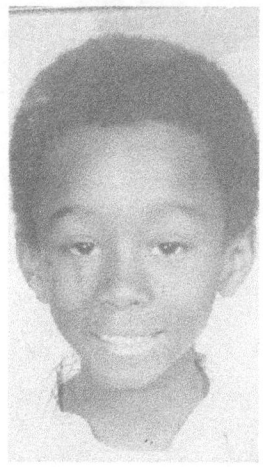

(Owner of Image: Gatlin, F.)

2 ~ The Hard Way

(Owner of Image: Gatlin, F.) Tom and Margie Rasco

Foster Youth

(Owner of Image: Gatlin, F.) Fourth Grade Jheri Curl

I really did not know how good I had it until I lied to my social worker about how I was being treated in the Rasco residence. My social worker came to see me one day, and for whatever reason (I may have been mad after getting a good butt whippin'), I told her that they only fed me rice and sometimes they made me sit under the sink. What?!

It made no sense at all! That was the furthest thing from the truth. I had to go and see a judge and explain to that man that I was lying. They almost took me out of my aunt's home. ATTENTION ALL FOSTER YOUTH: Listen, if you're a foster youth reading this and you're in a good home, please don't do or say anything stupid to mess things up.

When I look back and my childhood, I would not change one thing that happened to me and for me. Margie Rasco ruled the house with an iron fist, but I would not be the man I am today if it were not for her tough love and her dedication of always trying to teach me what was right.

I try my best to share my story with foster youth. Most of them don't get it, just like I didn't get it. I speak with kids who are stealing, getting high, getting bad grades, and hanging with the wrong crowd. I try to give them some words of wisdom before they completely blow their opportunity.

It's so hard for the agencies to place boys, especially black and brown boys. If you are a foster youth, please make the best of your situation. You need a stable environment so you can focus on being a kid and developing your mind. When you have a stable environment to live in, it takes away a lot of stress. You just have to remember to fight through the pain! It could be the pain of your parents abandoning you, the pain of a parent dying, the pain of being split up from your siblings, the pain of a learning disability, or even be the pain of being born addicted to crack cocaine. Whatever the pain may be, just know with God, prayer, and the help of good people, you will not have to fight through the pain alone. Seek out the help you need at all costs! Forgive those who did you wrong and prove to yourself and the world that you were not a mistake and you will make a difference in your world.

I fought through the anger of abandonment for years. I didn't forgive that person until I was thirty-six years old. Ironically, I found myself at church one day on Father's Day. The pastor asked every man in the building who was still holding resentment for anyone dead or alive to come down to the altar. So, I built up the courage to walk down. Before I knew it, I was at the altar hugging a stranger and crying in his arms.

The pastor said, "Forgive that person right now, and let it go."

I forgave that person that day and let all those years of anger drop off my shoulders. That moment allowed me to live a healthier emotional existence. That moment also helped me forgive and release other painful stressors that were holding me emotionally hostage for years.

Forgiving people is life-saving for you. Do it for yourself!

I'm So Skinny and Black ~ Can I Make It?

43

Greater Compton Panthers

(Owner of Image: Gatlin, F.) My second
year playing organized football.

Look at that smile and those chiseled arms. You can look at my arms and tell the guns were on their way. I had to start accepting who I was because my dark skin and skinny frame were all I had.

This was the organization where I started my football career. We were not that good, but we fought hard every week. We had good teams in our organization, but the teams I played on were just never that good. It was here where I started to gain a little confidence in myself as a football player.

Accepting who we are is the first step to greatness.

I Don't Want to Go to School Anymore ~ I Get Bullied Every Day

44

Stop It

The title of this chapter is not an excuse. This is just a cold hard fact for many kids all over the country. When I was in elementary school, I never told my aunt or any of my teachers about what was going on with me. I just took it upon myself one day at recess to bust the bully in the face with a basketball as hard as I could. He would push me and take my NFL pencils almost every day. I'm not overly proud of how I handled the situation, all I can say is that was the last day I was ever bullied. I don't recommend this action to any of my students. I'm just sharing what happened to me and what I chose to do about it.

If you are being bullied or your child is being bullied at school, please tell him or her to tell someone what's going on. This is the best way to fight back. If you have to literally fight back, then so be it! Just know that when you do literally fight back, there will most likely be consequences, especially if you seriously hurt the other person.

If no one knows what's going on, the abuse will continue in silence. Statistics say that one hundred thousand students stay home from school every day because of bullying. Suicide is the third leading cause of death among young people, and at least half of suicides among young people are related to bullying. It has to stop! This is definitely the number reason I do Bully Free workshops every year for my entire student body.

Some parents fear that if school administration confronts the bully after they have informed the school, the situation will get worse. In my experience as an administrator and teacher for the past twenty-four years, I've seen countless situations come to an end, once I met with both parents (separately) and had restorative justice meetings with the students involved. If your son's or daughter's school handles the situation correctly, the situation will eventually come to an end. If you are a parent with school-aged children, please start talking to them about how school is going on a daily basis. Bullying in person and cyberbullying, is a deadly game that we must stop together. The sixth-grade kid you see in the picture used to be one of those victims. Thank God he didn't have to deal with social media the way our kids do today.

Social Media

Parents, please start checking your kids' social media pages. Social media is the perfect breeding ground for bullies. As a school principal, I strongly suggest that parents of elementary and middle school students take away all access to Facebook, Instagram, Snapchat, Twitter, and texting. Flip phones will do the trick every time. *Yes*, I said it ... flip phones. Their primary function is to connect callers to engage in phone conversations. It's that simple. I know that might be too extreme for some parents, but sometimes being extreme is what needs to be done, if we want to help prevent our kids from being victims of bullies online and offline. Flip phone or no phone and limited access to the home computer is what I always suggest. If you're having social media problems with your kid, I say give it a try.

A Few Celebrities Who Were Bullied As Kids ~ If They Made It, Our Kids Can Make It

❖ Taylor Swift

- Tom Cruise
- President Barack Obama
- President Bill Clinton
- Tyra Banks
- Michael Phelps
- Chris Rock
- Lady Gaga
- Justin Timberlake
- Tiger Woods
- Eminem
- Duke of Sussex
- Khloé Kardashian
- Robert Pattinson
- Prince Henry
- Taylor Lautner

Sixth Grade Promotion ~ I made it! (Owner of Image: Gatlin, F.)

Speak up and speak often when you're being mistreated by anyone. If you don't, the madness will never stop.

They Booed Me ~ I Can't Go Back Out There

45

The Talent Show

The year was 1985. I was in the eighth grade at Roosevelt Junior High in Compton CA.. The talent show on campus was always the highlight of the year. So, my buddies and I agreed to try-out for the talent show as a popular singing group. You might have heard of them—a little group by the name of New Edition, only the most famous and popular boy band at the time. Members include the likes of, Ralph Tresvant, Bobby Brown, Johnny Gill (joined the group in 1987), Ricky Bell, Michael Bivins, and Ronnie DeVoe (also known as Bell, Biv, DeVoe). If you have no idea who this group is, please take some time to search and watch the *New Edition Story*.

So, we had three weeks to practice to get ourselves ready for the audition. After the first week, my buddies started getting cold feet. We hadn't even gotten one good practice in before everyone decided to quit. They said they couldn't do it. Now for whatever reason, I was the only fool who didn't quit. I said "Ya'll tripping! I'll just do it by myself." I don't know what I was thinking! Now how was I supposed to be a five-member group by myself?

Every day that went by, I managed to talk myself into auditioning. So, I practiced every day leading up to the audition. That day finally came, and it was on! I went in there, pushed play to "Lost in Love," and sang my heart out. At the end of the day, I had made the cut for the 1985 Roosevelt Junior High annual talent show.

The day of the show was finally here. I was wearing a white double-breasted suit with white shoes. I thought I was sharper than a knife at a blade convention. As I was backstage watching different acts go up, those dreaded words finally hit my ears: "You're next!" The act before me walked off stage, and the realization finally hit me that I was the next act up.

I grabbed the mic and waited patiently for the curtain to open. As the curtain opened, it seemed as if everything was in slow motion. The crowd was huge! It seemed like the entire school was out there watching. My heart was beating a million times per minute. As I stood there in fear, the music finally came on, and I started to sing. Once I opened my mouth, I was locked in! I thought I sounded pretty good, if you ask me.

All of a sudden, I started hearing people in the crowd shout out, "Sing, sing!"

I quickly realized that my mic was not on, and in the blink of an eye, I started hearing boos. I felt like I was at the Apollo. As soon as I started hearing the boos, I froze up, and the only thing that came out of my mouth was, "Damn!" As soon as I said damn, the damn mic cut on. I can still remember what seemed like an echo from hell roaring through the auditorium, "Damn, Damn, Damn, Damn ..." Everybody started laughing, and the only thing I could do at that point, was walk off stage.

A few acts went on after me, while I was backstage still in disbelief. All of sudden, I heard this chant from the crowd getting louder and louder. I looked out of the curtain and saw my boys getting it started. "We want Gat! We want Gat!"

I was absolutely terrified! One of the stage managers backstage walked up to me with a mic and said, "Are you going back out there?"

I had a quick second to think about it. I only had two choices. Run out of the back door as quick as possible or grab the mic and face the eight hundred some odd students chanting my name. And you know, 98 percent of them were not chanting my name because they wanted to hear me sing.

You know the majority them were chanting my name so they could get a second shot at booing at laughing at me.

I don't know what came over me, but in the blink of an eye, I just grabbed the mic and told them to cue up my tape. It seemed like the curtain opened in slow motion again. As soon as the music came on, the crowed got quiet. It was so quiet you could hear a mouse pee on cotton. As soon as the first words came out of my mouth, "Would you love me?" the girls started screaming and yelling, and my confidence just shot through the roof. I started pointing and moving my hips like I was Keith Sweat—and for you young folks, like I was Chris Brown. The more they screamed, the more confidence I gained. Before I knew it, I was in a zone, giving the audience all they could handle.

(Owner of Image: Gatlin. F.)

Roosevelt Middle School auditorium (Compton CA.), where the talent show went down.

That day changed my life forever. I was on the edge of disaster and kept my balance. My confidence has never been the same since. Before that day, I was kind of shy and quiet. After that day, everyone on campus knew who I was. In my mind, I was the man! When I walked around campus, people I didn't even know were speaking to me. "Eh, man, you were tight." "Hey,

Gat, you were up there doing it dog!" "There he is, girl! There he is!" It was a crazy experience. Like I said, my confidence soared to new heights. After that experience; I believed to my very core that I could do and accomplish anything I put my mind to. I figured if I could conquer that crowd of my peers (in the heart of Compton), I could conquer anything, anywhere, anytime, and any place. Some people may say it was just a silly talent show, but for me, it was a life-changing experience that needed to happen.

I started to become more confident in all of my classes. I was no longer afraid to give presentations in class. I was no longer afraid to speak to people I didn't know around campus, and I slowly became a leader. The next year I became the captain of our football team and basketball team, and I joined our ASB (Associated Student Body) class. We helped organize dances, ran the student store, and were responsible for the school newspaper and yearbook. Once I changed my mind-set, the sky was the limit.

Don't Love Me Like You Do ~ Talent Show Outfit 1985

(Owner of Image: Gatlin. F.) 8ᵗʰ Grade ~ Talent Show

You can take the easy road or the road that only a select few will take.

Can't Make Money
Like This Anywhere

46

Make This Quick Drop

(Owner of Image: Gatlin, F.)

I had a chance to make a quick drop of crack cocaine when I was fourteen years old. This older OG (original gangster) from the neighborhood came up to me and said, "Hey little homie, I need you to make a quick drop for me around the corner." He pulled the bag of rocks out of his pocket and dropped it in my hand.

I thought quick and hard. Flashes of my aunt whipping my behind, taking my football and basketball season away, and kicking me out of the house flashed through my head very quickly. I never once thought about the police. Those were the only thoughts I needed to stop me from becoming a potential dope dealer. I dropped the bag of rocks right back in his hands and said, "I'm cool!"

That was my first and last time ever being approached to make a drop or sell drugs. I believe that was a major turning point in my life. If I would've made that drop, who knows what that would've been the start of.

Short-Term Effects (According to Drug-Free World)

- Loss of appetite
- Convulsions, seizures
- Increased heart rate, blood pressure
- Panic and psychosis
- Contracted blood vessels
- Intense drug craving
- Nausea
- Anxiety, paranoia, and depression

Long-Term Effects

- Permanent damage to blood vessels of ear and brain
- Tolerance and addiction (from one hit)
- Liver, kidney, and lung damage
- Severe depression
- Malnutrition and weight loss
- Sexual problems, reproductive damage, and infertility
- Auditory and tactile hallucinations
- Respiratory failure
- Disorientation, apathy, and confused exhaustion

Drugs don't just kill people. They also kill dreams, potential, talent, careers, and families.

I'll Never Play Now

47

**Ebony and Ivory ~ Carson Colts ~ State Champions
1988 ~ Carson 55 versus Banning 7**

(Image taken by Leo Hetzel/*Press-Telegram*, 1988)
Fred Gatlin versus Perry Klien

Splitting time my senior year in high school with another quarterback was very difficult, especially when this other quarterback was an all-city quarterback from Palisades High School. A lot of people thought I would never play once he showed up. I knew in my heart I was not going to just give it to him. He would've had to kill me first. My life was dependent on this season. This season was do or die for me. It was scholarship or bust. This was the only year I was going to get an opportunity to play full-time varsity football to impress the college scouts.

Up to that point, in all of my years of playing sports, my aunt had never once came to a practice of mine to talk to a coach. She broke her streak in 1988. Her and my uncle Bubba came up to the school and had a serious conversation about my playing time with the Coach. I was somewhat embarrassed. I didn't want my teammates to think my "mommy" was at the school fighting my battles. I would soon realize, that conversation definitely needed to happen.

In the beginning of the season, this quarterback controversy divided the team and the community. This was a big deal for a few reasons.

1. He was white, and I was black.
2. He was rich, and I was not.
3. Our Carson High football team was nationally ranked in the top ten.
4. Our football team was in the championship game consistently for the past ten years.
5. We were always one of the top teams to beat in California.
6. Our team averaged five football scholarships a year.
7. It was senior year for the both of us.

This quarterback dual quickly started affecting the team. It got so bad at practice one particular day, that coaches had to stop practice. During an offensive play, Perry decided to keep the ball on an option play. He took about three steps, and it seemed like every player on the defense hit him as hard as they could. If you know anything about an offensive and defensive scrimmage at practice, the defense is never supposed to hit the quarterback.

I felt a little bad for him, but at the same time, I wasn't running to stop the madness.

If I can remember correctly, sometime after that practice, Perry quit the team and went back to Palisades High School. When he went back to ask his team and coach for forgiveness, they took a stance and felt he betrayed them. I don't know what other options he had after that. All I know is that he mustered up enough courage to come back to Carson.

When he came back, Coach Vollnogle (one of the greatness coaches in California high school history) made us apologize for the way we treated him before he left.

Before and during the season, things got kind of crazy with the local newspapers and television stations coming to our homes, the school, and the games (to interview people in the stands) regarding this big quarterback controversy.

As a team, we had to make some fast decisions. Either we were going to stay divided or come together as a team and make another run at the championship. Our talent level was neck and neck, so the Coach was forced to make a hard decision. The only thing Coach could do (that he thought was fair) was have us split time the entire football season. If I started one week, Perry would start the next. No matter who started the game, we would alternate every series throughout the duration of each game. I quickly realized that the conversation my aunt and uncle had with Coach, left a very strong impression.

Throughout the course of the season, the back and forth alternation killed our individual stats, but we both still managed to earn four-year scholarships. He went to Cal Berkley and soon after transferred to C.W. Post. And of course, I attended the University of Nevada, Reno (Wolfpack). Although both of us had to alternate the entire year, we still managed to lead our team to a 13–1 record and earn the right to be called state champions. We were one of the best teams in the state, and no one will ever be able to take that away from us for the rest of our lives.

This situation really taught me how to fight and never give up on my dreams—my dreams of becoming a starting quarterback in high school, college, and the pros. "I'll never play" entered my mind before the season started. But the more I thought about my future and how hard I fought to get to that point, I knew I had to fight to keep my dreams alive. At that moment, I knew it was time for me to grind and fight. It was either lie down and quit or fight for my future. Did I want to share time? *No, sir!* But I knew I had to do what I had to do to make my dream a reality. I had to play lights out every time I stepped on the field. I had to be the most intense player on the field. I was not just fighting for a touchdown or a win each week; I was fighting for my life. I had no other option but to go hard every practice, every weight room session, and every play. I was not going to be denied.

I'm going to try my best to find some of my old Carson High School highlights, so you can see how talented our team was back in 1988. I'll keep you posted. YouTube, watch out!

The Four Horsemen ~ Carson Colts 1988

(Owner of Image: Gatlin, F.)

I apologize for this picture not being clear. The fact that it was taken at night does night help either. This was the only picture that I could find of us. After all these years, I still can't believe I found it.

- **Larry Billoups, #9** ~ One of the fastest running backs I've ever played with. Once he turned the corner, it was over! (Long Beach State ~ Track and Field)
- **Armin Youngblood, #5** ~ One of the most versatile and reliable players I've ever played with (running back, slot back, and

quarterback). Once the ball was in his hands, first downs and touchdowns were inevitable. (Fresno State)

- **Errol Sapp, #22** ~ One of the best running backs I've ever played with. He was Houdini in cleats. Some of the moves I saw him do on the field were breathtaking. (University of Arizona)
- **Fred Gatlin, #1** ~ That's me!
- **Perry Klien, #7** (Fifth horseman–not in photo) ~ If it were not for him, I would have never found out (so early) what I was truly made of; soft mud or hard rock. He forced me to eat, sleep, and breathe football every day. He forced me to be a better leader. He forced me to step out of the shadows and be seen. Perry Klien definitely brought the best out of me. Iron sharpened iron the entire season. I learned that season, if you want to be the best, you have to compete against the best. He also brought a few more college scouts to our games as well. If they saw him, they saw me.

If it were not for these five individuals (and our incredible linemen, of course), I would've had a very hard time reaching my ultimate goal of earning a full scholarship and winning a state championship.

arterback Fred Gatlin alternate

Watts Summer Passing League Games: June, 1988

When you see a crack in the door, kick it open and play at your best when your best is needed!

I'll Never Play in
College ~ I'm Not Ready

48

Part of the Pack ~ 1989–1992

(Owner of Image: Gatlin, F.) Calling signals versus Boise State.

POSITION	HT	WT	CLASS	HOMETOWN
Quarterback	6-2	180	Soph.	Compton, CA

1989 Media Guide at UNR ~ My inner Bobby Brown

Feeling It Making the Grab

This is me in the middle of the field. My roommate
(Treamelle Taylor) at Mackay Stadium, absorbing the
crowd. An amazing football player and friend.
(Owner of both Images: Gatlin, F.)

Again I say, please check out highlights on YouTube. "I'll never play in college," ran through my mind once, but I had to let it keep running clear out of my head and into the dirt. I worked my butt off during the off season to make it happen. I believed I would start as a true freshman, so I put in the work, and it came to pass. I became a starter after the third game of the season. I continued to fight and claw for my position the next four years. This experience taught me how to lead men when I was just a boy. It taught me how to persevere through adversity and bounce back when things were not looking good. I had my challenges, but I was able to push through the pain and make it out on top with my sanity intact.

One of the Best Comebacks in College Football History
Nevada Wolfpack versus Weber State ~ November 2, 1991

We were playing Weber State during my junior season, and we were 8–0 at the time. I was having a solid season, averaging three hundred passing yards per game and at least two touchdown passes per game. I was one of our team captains, and I was on top of the world before the game started.

First Half: On our opening drive, we drove straight down the field and scored a touchdown. It was expected because this is what we were doing all season. This is also what I expected because I expected nothing less from myself but greatness.

After that first drive, for whatever reason, I just could not find my rhythm. I could not get the offense moving down the field consistently to save my life. In the first quarter, I threw my first interception of the game. I quickly had to go to the sideline and shake it off. Hey, it happens. A few series later, I came out and threw another interception, so I went to the sideline again and shook it off. I looked at my top receiver (Bryan Reeves, former NFL player and Wolfpack Hall of Famer) and just shook my head because he was not able to play. He got himself suspended for the game for not making curfew the night before. Anyway, just like that, we found ourselves down 21–7. I came out the next series and was able to hit Chris Singleton (former MLB professional baseball player and current MLB commentator) for a sixty-four-yard touchdown. We pulled within seven points (21–14), and I started to feel like I was getting my groove back.

Weber State had a quarterback at the time by the name of Jamie Martin (former NFL quarterback with the Rams, Redskins, Jaguars, Jets, Saints, and 49ers), and he was on fire that day. He had already thrown two touchdowns in the first quarter, and he bettered that with three more touchdowns before the end of the half to put them up 42–14. Wow! It was not a good feeling, trust me. Being on the other side of a good butt whipping does not feel good at all. The only thing we were able to do consistently, was move the ball down the field in spurts, but we were never able to put anything together to keep up with them.

Late in the second half, we had a good drive going. We were moving the ball down the field with consistent run and pass plays. On this particular series, we were feeling pretty good about ourselves. We had just run a long successful run play, and momentum was in our favor. As we broke the huddle for the next play, I started reading the defense as I was walking up to the line of scrimmage. I felt confident in what I saw, so I started my cadence, and the ball was snapped. I dropped back to survey the field; I saw an open receiver, and I pulled the trigger. I threw a rocket straight down the field, and just like that, the ball was intercepted once again. That was the third interception of the game and the worst start to a game throughout my entire college career.

Weber State got the ball back, but our defense made a late stop, and it was time for the offense to hit the field once again. As I ran out on to the field this time, I surprisingly got booed! Yes, after throwing three interceptions and having the worst start to a football game in my career, our home crowd had the audacity to boo me. Of course, I was shocked because I had never, ever been booed before by a home crowd. Now that I think about it after all these years, I probably would have booed myself after that poor performance.

So, as I was running out to the huddle, I felt like I was running in slow motion as the boos rang out. It felt like all twenty thousand fans in attendance were inside of my helmet booing me as loud as they could. I was so used to cheers, playing well, and signing autographs after games, that the boos shook my ego to the core. I'll be honest with you; it was very hard for me to recover from that shocking public humiliation.

One day you're on the mountaintop, and in the blink of an eye, you're the mud underneath people's feet. I tried my best to stay focused, but I could not muster up any magic to lead us down the field for a score. Once again, we had to punt. This is the worst feeling I believe a quarterback or any athlete can experience when they're not playing well.

Second Half: At the start of the second half, Weber State got the ball first and drove straight down the field for yet another touchdown. The score was now 49–14. The game was out of reach, and fans were starting to leave the stadium. I had faith in myself that I could bring us back because I had done it once before during my freshman year against Northern Arizona. We had been down 31–10 midway through the second quarter of that game, and I led that comeback, rallying us back to a 52–45 win, finishing with 420 yards passing and five touchdowns.

Now, back to this game. Although I still had confidence in myself, Coach Ault felt it was time to make a change, and I was pulled. Into the game came our backup quarterback, Chris Vargas. I was upset, but I had to be supportive of Chris because (#1) he was my teammate, and (#2) he was just an all-around good guy.

As soon as he came in, a spark started. All of a sudden, our defense did not allow another score for the rest of the game. The offense started moving the ball, and the momentum turned into a snowball, which quickly turned into a Wolfpack avalanche. Great throws, great catches, and great runs by running backs brought us back to life. Before we knew it, it was 49–21. Minutes later, we scored again. Now it was 49–28. When the score changed to 49–35, you could feel the confidence on the sideline take a big shift, and the crowd started getting louder and louder.

It became very evident that our guys started to believe we had a chance to pull this thing off. Meanwhile, in my own head, I was happy that we were making a comeback, but at the same time, I was upset that I was part of the reason we were down by so much in the first place. I was still caught up in my own feelings, but I couldn't show it to anyone at the time. A small part of me wanted the game to end so I could stop my personal pain and humiliation.

Chris brought us back from a thirty-five-point deficit and threw for three hundred yards and two touchdowns, all in the second half. I wanted to hate him, but I couldn't. So, the biggest comeback in college history was in the making, and all I could do was watch from the sideline. By the end of the game, the record books were shattered. The comeback was complete. We magically won the game, 55–49—the biggest comeback in college history and I had nothing to do with it, except throw three small interceptions in the first half.

After that game, I had to split time with Chris for the rest of the season. My confidence was shattered. I let the crowd and the circumstances take the life out of me. I had to somehow fight and claw my way back to the confident player I once was when I first stepped on campus. After sulking for a few weeks and talking with some close teammates, I quickly realized that I had to fight for my position and for a potential shot at pro football for the rest of my career at Nevada.

Through it all, I became a stronger man, and ironically, after that 1991 season, I was voted Offensive MVP of the Year by my teammates. When my senior year rolled around, I was also voted Most Inspirational Player of the Year by my teammates. They had seen my struggles and my triumphs, and together, we did some great things throughout the years.

A lot of people don't know this, but I was actually the first African American quarterback to ever play at the University of Nevada-Reno, Colin Kaepernick (former NFL quarterback, cultural icon, and activist) was the second. It was an amazing ride—the good and the bad. So, I say this … If this kid from Compton CA. could do it, you can do it. Do what? Do it! Change your mind-set. Only you know what it is. Just know that in the midst of doing it, you will experience greatness and defeat, beauty and ugliness, along with memorable moments of courage and fear. You must go through this for true change and greatness to happen. To all of you athletes, believe in yourself. Work hard and create your own path.

Coach Gatlin's College Statistics (as of January 1992)

- 30 wins (four-year span)
- Team MVP 1989 and 1991
- Big Sky New Comer of the Year 1989 (eleventh in the nation in passing efficiency)
- Team captain 1991 and 1992
- 63 touchdown passes
- 8,312 career passing yards

- First of all time: longest touchdown pass from scrimmage (98 yards to Treamelle Taylor versus Montana, 1989)
- 3 conference championships 1990, 1991, and 1992
- Part of 1990 Hall of Fame team (runner-up in the Division IAA National Championship)

Hall of Fame Consideration

(Owner of Image: Gatlin, F.) One day?

There's been a strong push in Reno throughout the years for me to (individually) enter the Wolfpack Hall of Fame. The top portion of this picture is a title I cut out from an article that was written about me by Chris Murry from the *Reno Gazette* in 2014. Murry has written an article every year for the past five or so years based on all of the valid reasons I should be inducted into the Wolfpack Hall of Fame. I really appreciate the love he has shown me through the years. It's a great honor to even be considered. Maybe it'll happen one day?

Now, if I would've put in the extra work in the film room and studied the game the way I was supposed to, I know I would've been a better quarterback all around and probably wouldn't have left any room for doubt or doubters. So please study! Study some more, and then study some more. The more you know and understand about your given craft, the quicker you will be able to master it.

> *If you want success to rain down on you, you have to*
> *be ready and willing to deal with the mud.*
>
> ~ Denzel Washington

You'll Never Go Pro

49

Calgary Stampeders (CFL ~ Canadian Football League)

(Owner of Image: Gatlin, F.) My first and only bubble gum card.

Moment of Truth

It was my rookie year, and I had just walked into the locker room after our second preseason game. I had a horrible game. I couldn't do anything right that night. After the game, I was feeling sad and sorry for myself.

As I was sitting at my locker taking off my uniform, the GM (general manager) Roy Shivers (former NFL player for the St. Louis Cardinals 1966–1972) walked over to me. He stood over me and just gave me a quiet tongue-lashing that no one else could hear. I definitely was not expecting this from my GM. I'll give you the PG version. He said, "I brought your behind all the way out here, and you play like this?! Play like that next game, and we're going to ship your butt out of here!" Remember, that was the PG version. His words were definitely a lot more colorful than that! He said it in true Roy Shivers fashion, honest and straight to the point.

As crazy as it sounds, his post-game pep talk lit a fire under me. Roy was very direct and pulled no punches. That's what I liked about him. He said exactly what was on his mind and exactly what I needed to hear. I came back the next (and last) preseason game and played lights out. I played like my career depended on it, and it did. After that last preseason game, I was called into the head coach's office and told that I had made the team. I earned my spot and beat the third-stream quarterback out for the last quarterback spot on the team.

Milan, Italy

(Owner of Image: Gatlin, F.) Focused in Rome

After I left Calgary and had a brief stint in Las Vegas, I rebounded with the Milan Rhinos in Milan Italy (European Football League). I got a chance to play in Switzerland, Rome, and various other parts of Italy. I also got a chance to walk the streets of Venice, Bologna, and Rimini.

Half of my teammates were Italian players, so I had to learn how to call the plays in Italian. We had a lot of fun that year and actually made it to the second round of the playoffs. I played one year with this team and I must say, I had a ball. It was a once-in-a-lifetime opportunity. Every day I walked the city it was an adventure. They wanted me to come back for a second year, but they could not afford to pay me what I thought I was worth. I wouldn't change a thing! Remember, check out highlights on YouTube. Just type in "Fred Gatlin QB."

Follow your dreams, no matter how crazy they may seem to others.

No One From My Neighborhood Will Ever Make It to the NFL

50

No! No! No! ~ Not Today!

49ers at Seahawks (Owner of Image: DeShawn Shead)

DeShawn Shead is a perfect example of hard work and perseverance. He started off as an undrafted free agent in 2012. He humbly started off on the Seahawks practice squad. He kept grinding and never quit. Before you knew it, he was called up to play on special teams. He had a great attitude and never complained. He just kept going to work every day and kept working. He eventually worked his way onto the defense's nickel-and-dime packages. As he continued to work and play consistent defense, he slowly became a fixture on the Legion of Boom. He eventually worked his way to a starting position for the 2014 Super Bowl Champion Seattle Seahawks.

He always had a great attitude and has always been a great competitor. I coached Shead his tenth, eleventh, and twelfth grade years at Highland High School in Palmdale, California. If you (student athletes) search hard enough, I'm sure you'll be able to find someone from your city who played or is playing a professional sport. They sacrificed their time, body, and more time to reach their goals. Please study them and follow their lead.

(Owner of Image: Gatlin, F.) Shead and Coach Gat

Shead and I at his 2015 DeShawn Shead Skills Camp in Palmdale, California. Shead puts on a free summer football camp for more than two hundred student athletes every summer in his hometown. He also signed a

$3.35 million dollar deal with the Detroit Lions on March 14, 2018. As of 2019, he was back playing for the Seattle Seahawks. As of February 2020, he reported as being a free agent.

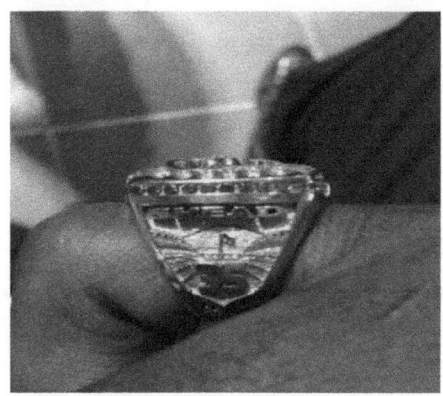 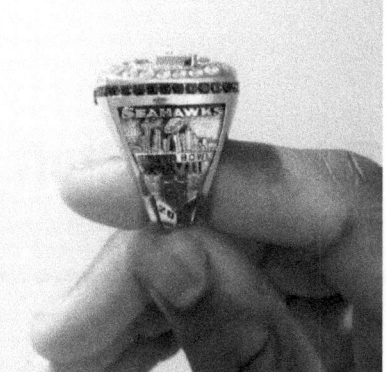

(Owner of Images: Gatlin, F.) Shead's Super Bowl ring

**Seattle Seahawks Super Bowl XLVIII ring.
Defeated the Broncos 43–8.**

This Acting Stuff Is Too Tough

51

Acting and Modeling Gallery

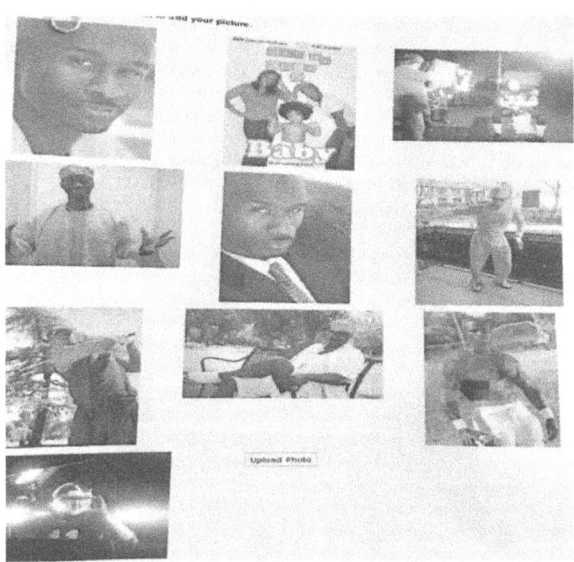

(Owner of Image: Gatlin, F.)

There is a lot that goes into being an actor and model. A lot of people don't know how challenging this business can be. I have much respect for every actor and model I set my eyes on—and not just those who have made it, but those who are still grinding on a daily basis, going to audition after audition, taking acting class after acting class, and getting rejection after rejection.

If you are an actor or an aspiring actor, please stick with it. Keep going to those acting, speech, and modeling classes. Study the business and study your craft. Every working actor has his or her horror stories of defeat and triumph. Stick with it so you can create your own.

Do not do what I did. I was going strong for about two years and I let my own thoughts and excuses get in the way.

- ❖ I'm tired of driving an hour every other day for a five-minute audition.
- ❖ I can't believe I didn't get that part. They are crazy!
- ❖ I need to make some money.
- ❖ There are too many actors out here.
- ❖ These acting classes are too expensive.
- ❖ What am I thinking?

The entire experience was tough but fun. I enjoyed it, but I eventually talked myself out of it. I had support from my wife and had a great teacher, but I got in my own way. I had the wrong mind-set.

I can never say I did not have a great teacher and supporting studio. Aaron Speiser, who has personally coached the likes of actors such as Will Smith, Gerard Butler, The Rock (Dwayne Johnson), Damon Wayans, Kim Wayans, and LL Cool J, is the most brutally honest teacher I've ever experienced.

He has an amazing acting studio (Speiser/Sturges Acting Studio) in Los Angeles. He is as real as they come. His acting classes were honest, and he taught simple life lessons every class. The first day of class he would let you know the unemployment rate for actors: 95–97 percent. "Does anyone want to go home now? This is your reality! Now let's work!" Every class, he would challenge you to dig deep within yourself, to figure out who you really were as a person. It is up to you and only you, if you want to be in that 1–5 percent of actors who are consistently working.

I can look back now and say I put in a little work, but I did not fight hard enough to maximize my acting potential. I worked for free on a few jobs. I landed a few gigs. I did a lot of extra work and earned my three SAG/AFTRA slips to be eligible to join the union. I met some great people and worked with an amazing teacher and studio. I will definitely revisit this chapter in my life one day. I have to. I owe it to myself. If you are an actor or aspiring actor, please do better than me. Exhaust all of the possibilities and all of your opportunities. Have no regrets!

Guilt

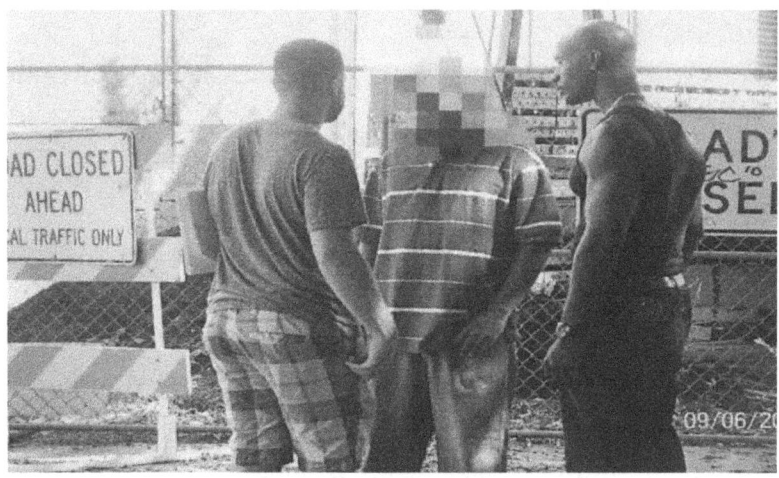

**(Owner of Image: Gatlin, F.) On set
working out a scene with a costar.**

This is a short film I did called *Guilt*. Here I am on set, discussing a scene with the director and the other actor (Vaughn T. Wilkinson). The film is about two childhood friends who become drug dealers. One friend wants to get out of the game, while the other has just begun. Chester (my character) does not want his friend to leave the game. Vaughn confesses to a priest about a crime he and Chester committed. Chester ends up shooting the priest in the mist of all of the drama, and in the end, he finds himself with a deadly bullet by a detective.

To prepare for this character, I wrote ten pages about Chester's life as soon as I got the part. I learned that strategy from acting class. It was my job to create a character who was real. He had to have a history and a life before the director said his first, "Action!"

I remember before we started shooting, I met with the director for coffee, and he ironically asked me about my character. He said, "Who is Chester?"

I was able to talk to him in detail about his mother, his father, his three brothers, and how he ran his drugs on the streets without getting caught. We spoke about Chester's life for about fifteen or twenty minutes. I was able to talk about Chester with confidence because he was a real person I'd created. He was no longer just a name in a script, he was me.

(Owner of Image: Gatlin, F.) *Guilt* ~ **Promotional Shot**

Year of the Quarterback ~ 2011 ESPN

**(Owner of Image: Gatlin, F.) Close-up shot of
me calling signals for a camera shot.**

This was a very fun experience for the simple fact that I played football all of my life. This shoot was for ESPN. They were shooting a slow-motion piece to open for a segment they were doing on quarterbacks. The show was hosted by Chris Connelly and a roundtable of experts such as Super Bowl coach John Gruden, Ron Jaworski, and Super Bowl champion and Hall of Famer Steve Young. This was a great documentary on the making of a quarterback and what makes a quarterback great. On the show they featured a variety of NFL quarterbacks from the past to the present.

We shot a lot of stills and a lot of slow-motion action shots. My favorite shoot was when they had me throw a football directly into the camera. The director had me stand about twenty yards from the camera and directed me to throw a tight spiral directly into the camera, which was protected by a thick piece of see-through fiberglass. I thought it would take me longer, but it only took me three shots to hit dead center into the camera lens. To make it happen, I really had to put some heat on the ball. When the ball hit the glass, it sounded like a bomb had gone off. *Boom!* As soon as the ball hit, the crew almost jumped out of their skin. We joked about that for about twenty minutes. Needless to say, they were able to get the shot they wanted. It was an all-around great experience for me. I will never forget it.

I Can't Coach Girls' Basketball

52

This team won thirty games in a row, spanning three
seasons and winning three championships.
[2017, 2018, and 2019]
(Owner of Image: Gatlin, F.)

If I'm being honest, I never wanted to coach girls' basketball. In my many years of coaching, I've found that girls are much more challenging to coach than boys. It all started for me in Compton back in 1997 at Roosevelt Junior High. We simply had no one who wanted to coach the girls' basketball team. The boys' team was already taken by a veteran coach, so the girls were all that were left.

I was hesitant at first, because I knew I would have to start from scratch. That meant teaching them how to dribble, how to shoot, how to play defense, how to comprehend different game strategies, and most importantly, how the rules of the game applied to them. What I quickly learned was that girls hang on to their emotions from earlier in the day and bring all of that drama into practice. I learned that I had to be a drill sergeant, if I wanted them to listen and respect the process.

I also learned that girls actually hang onto your every word, if you know what you're doing. You have to be organized, structured and know how to teach. With boys, they tend to think they know more than they actually do, so you have to stay on them like white on rice.

Because girls tend to listen more attentively, they learn much faster. So, before I knew it, I really started enjoying myself. They really started picking up the concepts of what I was teaching. Once I learned how to assess my talent and put in my press packages, it was off to the races. Once we started winning, it became an addiction for us all.

From 1997 until 2019, I have helped my girls' basketball teams win nine championships. We won four championships in Compton and five in Palmdale. I have learned to never say what I can't do. I know now that I can do anything I put effort and thought into. Sports saved my life, so I'm very happy I've had the opportunity over the years to pay it forward, teaching discipline, dedication, and work ethic to so many young ladies, as well as young men.

(Owner of Image: Gatlin, F.) 2015–2016 Championship Team

(Owner of Image: Gatlin, F.) Banners Equal
Championships ~ 2015-2016-2017-2018-2019

They Won't Get This Independent Living Stuff

53

Never underestimate kids. They are very resilient. I learned some great independent living skills when I was in a foster youth program my senior year in high school. I didn't think middle school kids would get it. I'm glad I didn't listen to myself and this horrible excuse. Over the past few years, students have come back to thank me for all of things they learned and experienced in my classes.

This independent living program was something I felt needed to be done. The program used to run once a month on Saturdays throughout the school year. I now teach the class twice a month during the week. My program teaches students lessons and skills that they do not get in regular school. We create activities and teach subjects such as budgeting, mock interviews, goal setting, vision boards, public speaking, argue and debate, spoken word, team building, how to tie a tie, interest rates on homes, tax brackets, home and apartment comparisons, and college and career research. We also take field trips to the Latino and Black College Expo every year.

(Owner of Image: Gatlin, F.)

Students enjoying the Black College Expo. (Los Angeles, California)

(Owner of Image: Gatlin, F.)

Coach Gatlin's Independent Living Program
~ Restorative Learning Circle

Independent Living Team-Building Activities

(Owner of Image: Gatlin, F.)

Me teaching team building concepts. They actually got it!

(Owner of Image: Gatlin, F.)

I Can't Win a Golf Tournament

54

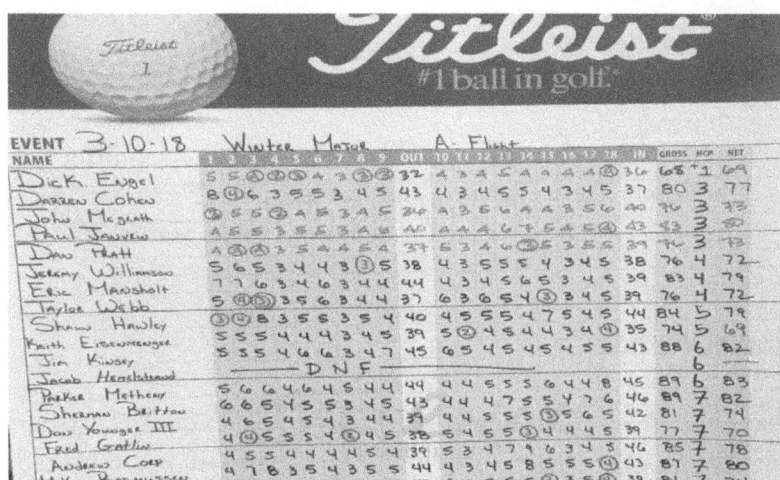

Shot a 77 to take third place in this tournament—Rancho
Vista Palmdale Men's. First and only time I've ever placed
in a tournament. (Owner of Images: Gatlin, F.)

Mike Rasmussen 5 6 5 3 4 5 3 6 5 42 6 3 5 5 5 5 ... 51 61 7 14
Wayne Allard 5 5 5 3 4 5 3 4 5 39 7 4 4 5 4 4 ②5 7 42 81 7 74
Joel Burch 4 6 5 4 4 4 5 4 5 41 4 3 4 5 5 4 3 5 ④ 37 78 7 71
Kenny Reynolds ③ 5 ④ 3 5 ② 3 4 5 35 A 3 4 6 4 4 3 5 6 39 74 4 70
Alex Massari 4 ④ 5 ② 4 5 4 4 5 37 5 ② 5 ④ 4 4 3 4 ④ 35 72 1 71
Bayardo Lopez

1st Gross # 100 - Dick Engel
1st Net # 100 - Keith Eisenmenger
2nd Net # 80 - Alex Massari
3rd Net # 60 - Fred Gaitlin

I did win a four-man scrabble with two of my golfing buddies. These two guys can flat-out play. We shot a 54 that day. Drop the mic! (Owner of Image: Gatlin, F.)

Parallel Worlds

What I love about golf is how parallel it is to life. It's literally a game that is filled with failure. But no matter how much you fail, you only need one good shot to give you confidence to come back for more. In life, we only need one yes, one person to forgive us, one opportunity, one break, one job, one meeting, one audition, one loan, or one prayer answered to change our day, our week, our month, or our lives.

Golfers call it a game of misses. The key is to have good misses. There are obstacles and traps all around the course just as there are traps and obstacles at the job, at home, and in the streets. The way you attack or avoid those obstacles, will determine the type of person you will be and become on any given day.

You're oftentimes one decision away from a great shot or disaster. When you do make mistakes, you have to forgive yourself and move on to the next shot. You have to continue to trust in yourself and trust in your shot. If you second-guess your decision, bad things usually happen. If you ever have a chance to experience having a good caddie on a premier golf course, please listen. In life, caddies come in the form of wives, husbands, best friends, mothers, teachers, coaches, counselors, fathers, siblings, children, and mentors.

In golf, if you practice the right things, you will get better. If you practice the wrong things or don't practice at all, your game will stay where it is, and you will never get better. Course management is critical. The more you can think your way around the course, the better round you will have. When frustration and anger show their ugly heads, you must control those emotions, or they will take over your day and you will have many regrets and frustrations. Uncontrolled emotions at home or at work, could potentially cost you your job or the trust of key relationships.

The golfer who makes the best and most consistent decisions always scores well. The golfer who knows how to control his or her emotions will be rewarded often. The golfer who learns how to forget about a previous bad shot and quickly become focused for the next shot, will also score well.

Golfers should consistently work on all aspects of their game (short game, putting, driver, long irons, bunker play, bump and run, flop shots, draws, cuts, and midirons). If they don't, their weaknesses will show up at the most critical times throughout any round. As human beings, I believe we must continue to be lifelong learners and lead learners, if we want to continue to grow as human beings.

Some days, golfers just don't play well, but they must learn how to forget about those days and create a new mind-set for the next time they go out to play. Just like in everyday life, we are not going to be at our best day in and day out, but we must continue to work on mastering ourselves daily.

There are always decisions that must be made. You can never get around that fact. Just like the many important decisions we must make in the course of a twenty-four-hour day, many decisions must be made in the course of a four-hour round of golf. Here are a few:

❖ Flop shot or bump and run?

- Should I put the ball in the front, back, or in the middle of my stance?
- Is the ball below or above my feet?
- Is it an uphill or downhill lie?
- Should I hit a draw or a fade?
- Is the wind blowing at my back, left to right, in my face, or right to left?
- Should I hit a punch shot?
- Should I hit it low or high?
- Should I close or open my club face?
- What's the distance?
- What type of grass is this?
- Are the grains of grass leaning with or against the roll of the putt?
- Is this green fast or slow?
- Should I keep my putter at 4 degrees, or should I change it to 2 degrees?
- What club should I use?

These are just a few decisions of many that must be made. Again, you must keep your emotions in check. High emotions are the enemy. It's so hard to win in the game of golf, but you just can't stop believing in yourself. A good golfer knows he or she must win one shot at a time and keep coming back for the competition and the excitement that each shot brings. Just like everyday life, we can only win one day at a time.

Hopefully (with the help of all of the pictures), you have a little better understanding of who I am and the foundation I came from. I truly believe pictures are worth a million words, and I hope they spoke to you in a million ways. I've been through a few things. I've done a few things, and I've left a few things unfinished. I have a lot more things to do, and I hope you do as well. Hopefully, you will start or continue to picture yourself doing great things for the rest of your life.

Make the rest of your life, the best of your life.
~ Dr. Eric Thomas

Excuses

55

I hope you were able to use something in these small chapters for yourself or someone else. I wanted to share with you some of my thoughts on different excuses I've used over the years. I also wanted to share a few excuses I've heard students and adults share with me as well. Through my experience working with different groups of people, we all try to protect ourselves and create a comfort zone as much as we can, even if that comfort zone is holding us back from successful productivity. Lastly, I wanted to share inspiring quotes, advice, and stories about different people who have made an impact in my life and the lives of so many around the world.

I definitely wanted to be transparent about myself with a few of my journeys and experiences over the years. I wanted to share a few intimate details about myself so you can see that we all go through similar experiences and that I'm not speaking at you but fighting alongside of you. Hopefully, some of my experiences will inspire and give you courage to change your mind-set. Sports helped change my life, and hopefully, some of the stories that you read resonated with you and inspired you in some way.

Training our mind-set is not a sprint workout. It's a marathon race that never ends until the clock strikes 00:00. We have to take control and consciously work to train our mind-set each and every day. We have to battle with our emotions, challenging circumstances, and old habits on a daily basis. We must allow the training field to mold and shape us every day. But it's up to us what direction our training will take us. The training is always going to be tuff and painful if our vision is worth creating.

As long as we live, we will continue to fight against excuses. Let's get in the habit of winning more fights than we lose. Like you, I have a lot of journeys that have shaped my life up to this point, and I have a lot more journeys that have yet to begin. I will continue to fight against excuses every time they show their ugly heads, and I hope you and those you care about continue to fight against these ugly lies for the rest of your lives as well.

Remember the two friends that live inside of us. Which one will eat, and which one will you starve?

Excuses are tools of incompetence, built on monuments of nothing.
~ Omega Psi Phi Fraternity, Inc. 1911

Something for you to think about as a reader is that there are two types of people in this world: those who read books like this and do nothing and those who put what they read into practice and enjoy immediate results.
~Phil M. Jones

~Notes~

Chapter 3 ~ I'm Too Tall: Young Ladies

1. The Office of Barack and Michelle Obama, Retrieved February 15, 2019 from https://barackobama.com/
2. Michelle Obama. (n.d.) In *Wikipedia*. Retrieved October 18, 2018 from https:// en.m.wikipedia.org/wiki/Michelle _Obama.
3. Beyoncé Knowles. (n.d.) In *Wikipedia*. Retrieved October 18, 2018, from https:// sco.m.wikipedia.org/wiki/Beyonce_Knowles.
4. Grammy.com March 17, 2014. Retrieved October 7, 2018
5. Serena Williams. (n.d.) In *Wikipedia*. Retrieved October 18, 2018 from https:// en.m.wikipedia.org/wiki/Serena_Williams.
6. Rankine, Claudia (August 25, 2015). "The Meaning of Serena Williams" The New York Times. Retrieved October 8, 2018 from https://nytimes.com/2015/08/30/magazine/the-meaning-of-serena-williams.html.
7. Venice Williams. (n.d.) In *Wikipedia*. Retrieved October 18, 2018 from https:// en.m.wikipedia.org/wiki/Venus_Williams.
8. "Venus Williams Biography" Biography. (January 19, 2018) Retrieved October 18, 2018 from https://biography.com /athlete/ venus-williams.
9. Candace Parker. (n.d.) In *Wikipedia*. Retrieved October 18, 2018 from https:// en.m.wikipedia.org/wiki/Candace Parker.
10. Biography Today Detroit, Michigan: Omnigraphics. 2010 pg. 143-46

11. Oprah Winfrey. (n.d.) In *Wikipedia*. Retrieved October 18, 2018 from https:// en.m.wikipedia.org/wiki/Oprah_Winfrey.

12. "The World's Most Powerful Celebrities," *Forbes*. Oprah Winfrey: A Biography, Second Edition by Helen S. Garson, Pg. 34-38 Retrieved October 18, 2018.

13. Rihanna. (n.d.) In *Wikipedia*. Retrieved October 17, 2018 from https:// en.m.wikipedia.org/wiki/Rihanna.

14. Natalie Robehmed, "How Rihanna Created a $600 Million Fortune-And Became The World's Richest Female Musician," *Forbes*. Retrieved July 17, 2019 from https://forbes.com/site/natalierobehmed/2019/06/04/rihanna-worth-fenty-beauty/#5cl6fco13de

15. Lisa Leslie. (n.d.) In *Wikipedia*. Retrieved October 17, 2018 from https:// en.m.wikipedia.org/wiki/Lisa Leslie.

16. "Lisa Leslie Biography" Black Book Partners, 2008. Retrieved October 20, 2018 from https://jockbio.com/Bios/Leslie/Leslie_bio.html

17. Queen Latifah. (n.d.) In *Wikipedia*. Retrieved October 18, 2018 from https:// en.m.wikipedia.org/wiki/Queen_Latifah.

18. Jason Buchanan, Allmovie (2008). "Queen Latifah: Biography. Retrieved October 18, 2018.

Chapter 4 ~ It Takes Too Long

1. "Work." Dictionary.com. 2019 https://www.dictionary.com (8 January 2018)

2. "Dedication." Dictionary.com. 2019 https://www.dictionary.com (8 January 2018)

3. "Pain." Dictionary.com. 2019 https://www.dictionary.com (8 January 2018)

4. "Suffering." Dictionary.com. 2019 https://www.dictionary.com (8 January 2018)

5. "Develop." Dictionary.com. 2019 https://www.dictionary.com (8 January 2018)

6. "Grow." Dictionary.com. 2019 https://www.dictionary.com (8 January 2018)

7. "Labor." Dictionary.com. 2019 https://www.dictionary.com (8 January 2018)

8. "Fruit." Dictionary.com. 2019 https://www.dictionary.com (8 January 2018)

9. "Sacrifice." Dictionary.com. 2019 https://www.dictionary.com (8 January 2018)

Chapter 5 ~ I Need My Sleep

1. "There Is No Tomorrow." Rocky III, R. Chartoff and I. Winkler, (Producer) Sylvester Stallone (Director). (1982) [Motion Picture] United State: MGM/UA Entertainment Co.

2. "Broke." Dictionary.com. 2019 https://www.dictionary.com (8 January 2018)

Chapter 6 ~ Everyone Will Thinks I'm Crazy

1. "Years of Athletic Achievement," davidgoggins.com. Retrieved March 12, 2019, Pg. 3-4

2. "The Wright Brothers & the Invention of the Aerial Age," Smithsonian Institution. August 13, 2015, Retrieved June 17, 2018 from https://airandspace.si.edu/exhibitions/wright-brothers/online/whol. Pg. 1-3

3. Eric Thomas. (n.d.) In *Wikipedia*. Retrieved August 12, 2018 from https:// en.m.wikipedia.org/wiki/Eric Thomas.

4. Robert Nay. (n.d.) In *Wikipedia*. Retrieved October 16, 2018 from https:// en.m.wikipedia.org/wiki/Robert Nay.

5. Jones, Sam (18 January 2011). "Angry Brids Knocked off perch by Bubble Ball." London: Guardian.co.uk. Retrieved January 15, 2018 from https://www.theguradian.com/technology/2011/jan/18/angry-bird-bubble-ball-itunes.

6. "Robert Nay, Bubble Ball: A 14-Year-Old Built The No. 1 IPhone Game." Huffington Post, August 9, 2011. Retrieved January 16, 2018 from https://www.huffpost.com/entry-nay-bubble-ball-14-year-old-built-iphone-app-n-91070

7. "Who is C.T.? The Original Iron Addict," Retrieved August 12, 2018 from https://ctfletcher.com/

8. Barack Obama. (n.d.) In *Wikipedia*. Retrieved January 21, 2018 from https:// en.m.wikipedia.org/wiki/Barack_Obama.

9. "President Barack Obama." The White House. 2008. Retrieved January 21, 2018 from https://web.archieve. org/web/20091026043047/http://www.whitehouse.gov/ administration/president-obama.

10. "The Three Doctors, Our Story," threedoctors.com, Retrieved August 11, 2018 from www.threedoctors.com

11. Arnold Schwarzenegger. (n.d.) In *Wikipedia*. Retrieved August 13, 2018 from https:// en.m.wikipedia.org/wiki/Arnold_ Schwarzenegger.

12. L. Leamer, *Fantastic: The life of Arnold Schwarzenegger*. (St Martin's Press, 2005), Retrieved August 13, 2018. Pg. 67-81

13. Thomas Edison. (n.d.) In *Wikipedia*. Retrieved August 13, 2018 from https:// en.m.wikipedia.org/wiki/Thomas_Edison.

14. Anna Sproule, *Thomas Alva Edison: The Worlds' Greatest Inventor* (1st US ed.). (Woodridge, CT: Blackbirch Press, 2000), Retrieved August 13, 2018.

15. Lewis Latimer. (n.d.) In *Wikipedia*. Retrieved August 13, 2018 from https:// en.m.wikipedia.org/wiki/Lewis_Latimer.

16. "Lewis H. Latimer Dead. Member of Edison Pioneers. Drew Original Plans for Bell Phone," *New York Times*. December 13, 1928. Retrieved August 13, 2018.

17. "Black Excellist:10 Young Black Entrepreneurs & Millennials." Youtube. Video Length 8:40. www.blackexcellist.com. April 4, 2018. Retrieved from https://youtu.be/ XDI0nIZA68.

18. "Misty Copeland." The Official Website of Misty Copeland. Retrieved March 3, 2020 https://www.mistycopeland.com

Chapter 7 ~ I Don't Have Any Time

1. "Freedom." Dictionary.com. 2018 https://www.dictionary.com (11 January 2018)

2. "Time." Dictionary.com. 2018 https://www.dictionary.com (11 January 2018)

Chapter 8 ~ It's Too Hard

1. "Hard." Dictionary.com. 2018 https://www.dictionary.com (11 January 2018)

Chapter 9 ~ The Odds Are Too Great: Athletes

1. "Estimated Probability of Competing in College Athletics," NCAA. org, April 3, 2019. Retrieved April 28, 2019 from www.ncaa.org/about/research/estimated-probability-competing-college-athletics.
2. R. Donner, O. Stone, D. Halsted, L. Donner, and C. Townsend, (1999) *Any Given Sunday* [Motion Picture] United States: Warner Bros. Pictures.
3. "Perseverance." Dictionary.com. 2019 https://www.dictionary.com (12 January 2018)
4. "Champion." Dictionary.com. 2019 https://www.dictionary.com (12 January 2018)

Chapter 11 ~ The System Is Not Designed For Me (African American Golf Legends)

1. P. McDaniel, (2000) *Uneven Lies-The Heroic Story of African-Americans in Golf.* Greenwich Connecticut: The American Golfer. Pg. 23, 75-76, 85-93, 101-108, 136-138.
2. George Franklin Grant. (n.d.) In *Wikipedia.* Retrieved May 24, 2019 from https:// en.m.wikipedia.org/wiki/George Franklin_ Grant.
3. "African American and the Game of Golf" African American Registry. *New York Times.* Retrieved May 24, 2019 from https://aaregistry.org/story/african-americans-and-golf-a-brief-historty/
4. Ben Hogan. (n.d.) In *Wikipedia.* Retrieved May 24, 2019 from https:// en.m.wikipedia.org/wiki/Ben_Hogan.

5. The Hard Life of a Golfing Great," *Bloomberg Businessweek*. (June 18, 2004). Retrieved May 24, 2019 from https://www.bloomberg.com/news/article/2004-06-17 the-hard-life-of-a-golfing-great.

6. Tiger Woods (n.d.) In *Wikipedia*. Retrieved May 15, 2019 from https://en.m.wikipedia.org/wiki/Tiger_Woods.

7. Jaime Diaz, "What Made Tiger Woods Great-And Can Again-Golf Digest," *Golf Digest*. Retrieved May 15, 2019 from https://www.golfdigest.com/story/what-made-tiger-woods-great-and-can-again-jaime-diaz-magazine.

8. "Expensive." Dictionary.com. 2018 https://www.dictionary.com (14 January 2018)

9. Calvin Peete. *In Wikipedia*. Source: Calvin Peete 1986 Western Open. Author: Ted Van Pelt. Retrieved June 9, 2019.

Chapter 12 ~ It's Too Expensive

1. "Believe." Dictionary.com. 2018 https://www.dictionary.com (14 January 2018)

Chapter 15 ~ I Need More Sleep

1. Samuel Jackson. (n.d.) In *Wikipedia*. Retrieved December 3, 2018 from https:// en.m.wikipedia.org/wiki/Samuel_Jackson.

2. Lindsay Powers, "Samuel L. Jackson Is Highest Grossing Actor of All Time," *The Hollywood Reporter*. (October 27, 2011) Retrieved December 3, 2018 from www.hollywoodreporter.com/news/samuel-l-jackson-highest-grossing-actor-guinness-book-world-records-254155

3. Fauja Singh. (n.d.) In *Wikipedia*. Retrieved December 3, 2018 from https:// en.m.wikipedia.org/wiki/Fauja_Singh.

4. Ray Kroc. (n.d.) In *Wikipedia*. Retrieved December 3, 2018 from https:// en.m.wikipedia.org/wiki/Ray_Kroc.

5. Robert Anderson, "Ray Kroc How He Made McDonald's Sizzle," *Success*. (March 2009) Retrieved December 3, 2018 from https://www.thefreelibrary.com/Ray+Kroc%3A+howthe+made+McDonald%27s+sizzle.-a0206252545

6. Taikichiro Mori. (n.d.) In *Wikipedia*. Retrieved December 3, 2018 from https:// en.m.wikipedia.org/wiki/Taikichiro_Mori.

7. Stan Lee. (n.d.) In *Wikipedia*. Retrieved December 3, 2018 from https:// en.m.wikipedia.org/wiki/Stan_Lee.

8. Allison Kugel, "Stan Lee: From Marvel Comics Genius t Purveyor of Wonder with POW! Entertainmnet." PR.com. (March 13, 2006) Retrieved December 3, 2018 from https://www.pr.com/article/1037

9. Colonel Sanders. (n.d.) In *Wikipedia*. Retrieved December 5, 2018 from https:// en.m.wikipedia.org/wiki/Colonel_Sanders.

10. Harland Sanders, *The autobiography of the Original Celebrity Chef.* (Louisville: KFC, 2012) Retrieved December 5, 2018 from https:// kfc.bg/biografia.pdf. Pg. 10-32, 23-32, 50-52, 65-70.

11. Sylvester Stallone. (n.d.) In *Wikipedia*. Retrieved December 5, 2018 from https:// en.m.wikipedia.org/wiki/Sylvester_Stallone.

12. "Sylvester Stallone: Director, Producer, Screenwriter, Actor, Film Actor (1946-)," Retrieved December 5, 2018 from https:// biography.com/actor/sylvester-stallone.

Chapter 26 ~ I Don't Feel Like It

1. LDF, "The Significance of 'The Doll Test," Retrieved April 27, 2019 from https://www.naccpldf.org/ldf-celebrates-60th-anniversary-brown-v-board-education/signifcance-doll-test.

Chapter 27 ~ My Skin Is Too Dark

1. T. Kenneth, "Ava DuVerany's documentary '13th' simmers with anger and burns with eloquence" https://www.latimes.com. (October 6, 2016) Retrieved June 8, 2019

2. *13th* Netflix, Director: DuVernay, A., Producer: DuVernay, A., Averick, S., Barish, H., September 30, 2016. Production Company: Kandoo Films

Chapter 34 ~ I Can't Handle Failure

1. ESPN Statistics, 2019. ESPN Internet Ventures. Retrieved from June 20, 2019 from www.espn.com/mlb/stats/batting.

Chapter 38 ~ I'm Not a Leader

1. Habits for Wellbeing, "6 Core Human Needs by Anthony Robbins," Retrieved November 19, 2018 from https://habitsforwellbeing.com/6-core-human-needs-by-anthony-robbins.
2. "Therapy in America," American Psychological Association, *Psychology Today Magazine* & Pacific Care Behavioral Health (May 2004).
3. "Praise." Dictionary.com. 2018 https://www.dictionary.com (10 April 2018)
4. "Reprimand." Dictionary.com. 2018 https://www.dictionary.com (10 April 2018)

Chapter 39 ~ The Odds are too Great, Part II: A Football Life

1. Doug Williams. (n.d.) In *Wikipedia*. Retrieved March 8, 2019 from https:// en.m.wikipedia.org/wiki/Doug_Williams.
2. Sander Philipse, "Doug Williams inducted into Black College Football Hall of Fame," BucsNation.com. (February 20, 2011) Retrieved March 8, 2019 from https://www.bucsnation.com/2011/2/20/2004349/doug-williams-induction-into-black-college-football-hall-of-fame.
3. Marlin Briscoe. (n.d.) In *Wikipedia*. Retrieved March 8, 2019 from https:// en.m.wikipedia.org/wiki/Marlin_Briscoe.
4. "Briscoe Fourth Hall of Famer," *The Gateway Newspaper*. (November 7, 1975) Retrieved March 8, 2019. Hall of Fame. "Marlin Briscoe" Retrieved March 8, 2019 from https://footballfoundation.org/hof_search.aspx?hof=2389
5. Warren Moon. (n.d.) In *Wikipedia*. Retrieved March 8, 2019 from https:// en.m.wikipedia.org/wiki/Warren_Moon.
6. "Warren Moon," Contemporary Black Biography. (The Gale Group, Inc., 2006) Retrieved March 8, 2019.

7. James Harris. (n.d.) In *Wikipedia*. Retrieved March 10, 2019 from https:// en.m.wikipedia.org/wiki/James_Harris.

8. Samuel G. Friedman, "The quarterback who paved the way for Colin Kaepernick's protests," *The Washington Post*. (February 2, 2018) Retrieved March 10, 2019 from https://www.washingtonpost.com/news/made-by-history/wp/2018/02/02/the-quarterback-who-paved-the-way-for-colin-kaepernicks-protests/

9. Steve McNair. (n.d.) In *Wikipedia*. Retrieved March 10, 2019 from https:// en.m.wikipedia.org/wiki/Steve_McNair.

10. "Remembering Air McNair – NCAA Football," Sporting News. Retrieved March 10, 2019.

11. Randall Cunningham. (n.d.) In *Wikipedia*. Retrieved March 10, 2019 from https:// en.m.wikipedia.org/wiki/Randall_Cunningham.

12. Michael Vick. (n.d.) In *Wikipedia*. Retrieved March 12, 2019 from https:// en.m.wikipedia.org/wiki/Michael_Vick.

13. "Michael Vick Biography," Biography.com. Retrieved March 12, 2019 from https://www.biography.com/athlete/michael-vick.

14. Russell Wilson. (n.d.) In *Wikipedia*. Retrieved March 12, 2019 from https:// en.m.wikipedia.org/wiki/Russell_Wilson.

15. "Russell Wilson, QB for the Seattle Seahawks at." Nfl. com. Retrieved March 12, 2019 from www.nfl.com/player/russellwilson/2532975/profile

16. Joe Gilliam. (n.d.) In *Wikipedia*. Retrieved March 12, 2019 from https:// en.m.wikipedia.org/wiki/Joe_Gilliam

17. "Jow Gilliam Jr. had athletic leadership skills," The African American Registry Retrieved March 12, 2019 from https:// aaregistry.org/story/joe-gillian-jr-had-athletic-leadership-skills/

18. Donavan McNabb. (n.d.) In *Wikipedia*. Retrieved March 12, 2019 from https:// en.m.wikipedia.org/wiki/Donavan_McNabb.

19. "Donovan McNabb: Careee Stats." NFL. NFL Enterprises. Retrieved March 12, 2019 from www.nfl.com/player/donovanmcnabb/250244/careerstats

20. Goodread, Chase (September 17, 2016). "Lamar Leads accounts for five TDs in 63-20 rout FSU. NFL.com. Retrieved October, 2019

21. Culpepper, Chuck (December 10, 2016) "Lamar Jackson's Heisman Trophy triumph a story over 20 years in the making. The Washington Post. Retrieved December 4, 2019.

22. Baltimore Ravens, Lamar Jackson. ESPN. Espn.com. Retrieved December 10, 2019 from espn.com/nfl/game/_/gameld/401128020

Chapter 40 ~ Nothing Good Comes Out of the City of Compton

1. "Before the 1950s, the Whiteness of Compton was Defended Vehemently," http://www.kcet.org, Behrens, Z., (January 11, 2011) Retrieved June 2, 2019

2. "The Compton Clash: Race Relations." http://www. thecomptonclash.blogspot.com. http://projects.latimes.com/mapingla/neighborhoods/neighborhood/compton. Ramirez, L. 25th April 2012. Retrieved June 2, 2019.

3. "Compton California (1867-)" htpp://www.blackpast.org. August 20, 2017. Ayala F-H. Retrieved June 2, 2019.

4. B. Gann, (June 3, 2011). The Crips (1971-?). Retrieved from https://www.blackpast/aaw/vignette_aahw/crips-1971.

5. B. Gann, (June 9, 2011) The Bloods (1972-?). Retrieved from https://www.blackpast/aaw/vignette_aahw/bloods-1972.

6. S, Anjuli, "When LA Erupted In Anger: A Look Back At The Rodney King Riots," (April 26, 2017) Retrieved from https://www.kpbs.org. Retrieved June 3, 2019.

Chapter 46 ~ Can't Make Money Like This Anywhere

1. "Foundation For A Drug-Free World," Drugfreeworld.org. Retrieved May 26, 2019

Chapter 47 ~ I'll Never Play Now

1. L. Langlois and L. Hetzel, "What Quarterback Controversy," C1, C4, *Press-Telegram*, (December 8, 1988) Col. 1

Chapter 48 ~ I'll Never Play In College – I'm Not Ready

1. C. Murry, "Gatlin for HOF, Former Wolfpack Quarterback Deserving of Consideration for Hall of Fame Honor," *Reno Gazette Journal*, (May 11, 2014) C5.

**STRAIGHT
OUT OF
COMPTON**

Finished!

Lightning Source UK Ltd.
Milton Keynes UK
UKHW011832010420
361205UK00003B/17